Selling Sex

ISSUES

Volume 174

Series Editor

Lisa Firth

Independence

Educational Publishers

First published by Independence
The Studio, High Green
Great Shelford
Cambridge CB22 5EG
England

British Library Cataloguing in Publication Data
Selling Sex – (Issues; v. 174)
1. Sex-oriented businesses 2. Sex crimes 3. Children and sex
I. Series II. Firth, Lisa
363.4'4-dc22

ISBN-13: 978 1 86168 488 2

Printed in Great Britain
MWL Print Group Ltd

Cover
The illustration on the front cover is by
Angelo Madrid.

CONTENTS

Chapter One: Prostitution

Chapter Two: Pornography

Chapter Three: Sexualising Society

Useful information for readers

Dear Reader,

Issues: Selling Sex

Sexualised images seem to be everywhere in our society: in advertising, in magazines and on television. But is the sex industry as glamorous as such images might lead us to believe? This title looks at how both the act and the idea of sex are for sale in our society. It covers the debates surrounding prostitution, sex trafficking and pornography, as well as other areas of the sex industry such as lap dancing clubs. It also looks at the sexualisation of society.

The purpose of *Issues*

Selling Sex is the one hundred and seventy-fourth volume in the **Issues** series. The aim of this series is to offer up-to-date information about important issues in our world. Whether you are a regular reader or new to the series, we do hope you find this book a useful overview of the many and complex issues involved in the topic.

Titles in the **Issues** series are resource books designed to be of especial use to those undertaking project work or requiring an overview of facts, opinions and information on a particular subject, particularly as a prelude to undertaking their own research.

The information in this book is not from a single author, publication or organisation; the value of this unique series lies in the fact that it presents information from a wide variety of sources, including:

⇨ Government reports and statistics
⇨ Newspaper articles and features
⇨ Information from think-tanks and policy institutes
⇨ Magazine features and surveys
⇨ Website material
⇨ Literature from lobby groups and charitable organisations. *

Critical evaluation

Because the information reprinted here is from a number of different sources, readers should bear in mind the origin of the text and whether the source is likely to have a particular bias or agenda when presenting information (just as they would if undertaking their own research). It is hoped that, as you read about the many aspects of the issues explored in this book, you will critically evaluate the information presented. It is important that you decide whether you are being presented with facts or opinions. Does the writer give a biased or an unbiased report? If an opinion is being expressed, do you agree with the writer?

Selling Sex offers a useful starting point for those who need convenient access to information about the many issues involved. However, it is only a starting point. Following each article is a URL to the relevant organisation's website, which you may wish to visit for further information.

Kind regards,

Lisa Firth
Editor, **Issues** series

*Please note that Independence Publishers has no political affiliations or opinions on the topics covered in the **Issues** series, and any views quoted in this book are not necessarily those of the publisher or its staff.*

ISSUES TODAY
A RESOURCE FOR KEY STAGE 3

Younger readers can also now benefit from the thorough editorial process which characterises the **Issues** series with the launch of a new range of titles for 11- to 14-year-old students, **Issues Today**. In addition to containing information from a wide range of sources, rewritten with this age group in mind, **Issues Today** titles also feature comprehensive glossaries, an accessible and attractive layout and handy tasks and assignments which can be used in class, for homework or as a revision aid. In addition, these titles are fully photocopiable. For more information, please visit the **Issues Today** section of our website (www.independence. co.uk).

Prostitution

Information from politics.co.uk

What is prostitution?

Prostitution describes the offering and provision of sexual services for financial gain.

In the UK, prostitution itself is not illegal but there are a number of offences linked to it. For example it is an offence to control a prostitute for gain, or to keep a brothel.

Prostitution has a close affinity with a host of other important social issues, in particular crime, drugs, sexual equality, poverty and health.

Although there are exceptions, most prostitutes are women selling their services to men.

Background

Prostitution is sometimes referred to as 'the oldest profession', as it meets the natural urges of humans in return for money, and is often claimed to be as old as civilisation itself.

The legal regulation of prostitution in the UK was set out in the Sexual Offences Act 1956, which reflected the findings of the Wolfenden Committee investigation into prostitution and homosexuality that took place around that time.

The Wolfenden Committee treated prostitution and its status in the law as a moral issue and this was reflected in the text of the Act. This led to famous debates between Lord Devlin and the philosopher Herbert Hart.

In late 2003 the Home Office announced its intention to review the laws on prostitution with the aim of overhauling the dated regulations of the 1956 Act. Subsequently amendments relating to prostitution were made under the Sexual Offences Act 2003 with regard to the following offences; 'causing or inciting prostitution for gain', 'controlling prostitution for gain', 'penalties for keeping a brothel used for prostitution' and 'extension of gender-specific prostitution offences'.

The Policing and Crime Bill, introduced to the Commons in December 2008, creates a new offence of paying for sex with someone who is controlled for gain and introduces new powers to close brothels; it also modifies the law on soliciting. Following a Second Reading in January 2009, the bill was sent to a Public Bill Committee for scrutiny, due to be completed in February 2009*.

Controversies

As with all matters of sexuality, prostitution continues to be debated on both social and moral levels. Opponents of prostitution and moral conservatives believe the practice is intrinsically morally corrupt and a challenge to family values, therefore regarding a ban to be justified in the name of public morality. Many religious groups adopt this position, adding another aspect to the debate.

However, many who regard involvement in prostitution as a matter of private morality still argue for legal regulation.

Prostitution's quasi-criminal status has led it to be closely associated with organised crime, poverty, drugs, child abuse and people trafficking.

Virtual imprisonment has become a particular problem in recent years, notably since the fall of the Iron Curtain and the break-up of Yugoslavia. There has been an increase in the 'white slave trade' from Eastern Europe and Russia, along with a general influx of organised crime, with many women thought to be living as virtual slaves.

Because prostitutes have large numbers of sexual partners, they are more likely to have sexually transmitted infections and be vectors for spreading these infections – adding a public health dimension to the debate.

The Government says it wants to reduce prostitution in the UK and, as some say legal controls are too blunt a tool, is trying to establish what policies would work. For example, in 2002 the Government made a total of £850,000 available for groups working in a multi-agency context to implement local strategies for reducing prostitution-related crime and disorder.

Some argue that licensed brothels would help to ensure worker safety, keep them off the streets, help prevent health problems, bring revenue to the Treasury and remove the need for exploitative and abusive pimps. However, many others find this morally repugnant.

The murders of five prostitutes in Ipswich in November and December 2006 reignited calls for a new approach to tackling the issue.

There are estimated to be around 80,000 people involved in prostitution in the UK

In November 2008, the Home Office published the findings of a six-month review into how the demand for prostitution could be reduced. Home Secretary Jacqui Smith, in a foreword to the review, stated: 'So far, little attention has been focused on the sex buyer, the person responsible for creating the demand for prostitution markets. And it is time for that to change.'

But Government plans to create a new law under the Policing and Crime Bill making it an offence to pay for sex with someone who is 'controlled by another for gain' is causing particularly controversy. Even if the person paying for sex is unaware that the prostitute is trafficked or controlled by a pimp, they will still be liable for prosecution and if convicted will be given a criminal record and a fine of up to £1000.

The Bar Council has warned that the offence as currently drafted risks convictions that may be seen as unfair by reasonable people and that such convictions would bring the criminal law into disrepute, particularly given the stigma that would result.

Concerns have also been raised by several MPs including the Labour chair of the Home Affairs Select Committee, Keith Vaz, who said that he was 'not convinced that the best course of action is to prosecute in the proposed way men who go into situations where they wish to buy sex

from prostitutes'.

And Shadow Justice Minister, Henry Bellingham stated, 'We do not in any way want to stand up for the people who feel they have to, in unfortunate circumstances, go and use prostitutes. We are concerned, however, about bringing in credible law that will stand the test of being put through the courts.'

Statistics

⇨ There are estimated to be around 80,000 people involved in prostitution in the UK.

⇨ Research by the Poppy project identified 1500 establishments involved in the off-street sex industry in London alone.

⇨ The prostitution market in the UK is calculated to be worth up to £1bn, with estimates of the proportion of UK men paying for sex ranging from 4.3% to 11%.

Source: Home Office review 'Tackling the Demand for Prostitution' – November 2008

If convicted of kerb crawling you could face:

⇨ a £1000 fine;

⇨ losing your driving licence;

⇨ exposure of your habits to family, friends and work colleagues.

If convicted of paying for sex with someone who is under 18, you could face life imprisonment.

Source: homeoffice.gov.uk – 2009

Quotes

'There will be no more excuses for those who pay for sex. This new criminal offence of paying for sex with someone who is trafficked or pimped will apply even if the buyer claims he did not know the woman was being controlled for gain.

'I also want to tackle kerb crawling. In my book, once around the block is once too many, and so I'm making kerb-crawling punishable as a first offence. I also want to see more naming and shaming of persistent kerb crawlers.'
Home Secretary Jacqui Smith, Home Office press release – November 2008

'We entirely agree with the objective, but the proposed reforms will not achieve the desired outcome. They will drive sex workers underground, into less safety, more isolation and a

greater risk of disease. We will seek amendments.'
Liberal Democrat Home Affairs spokesman Chris Huhne, Commons debate – January 2009

'JUSTICE has not taken a position on the morality of prostitution but we believe that – as in the case of controlled drugs – while it is possible that legal prohibition may deter some men from using prostitutes, many others – in particular those with less respect for the law in general – will not be so deterred.'
Human rights organisation JUSTICE, briefing on second Commons reading of Policing and Crime Bill – January 2009

'Kerb crawling fuels the exploitation of women by indirectly supporting drug-dealers and abusers. If you frequent prostitutes, you could be contributing to the violence and abuse these women already face, often against their will.'
homeoffice.gov.uk – 2009

'We oppose the government's proposals which would create new offences relating to: 1) paying for sex, 2) brothel keeping, and 3) kerb crawling. It is clear that the intention is to target anyone involved in prostitution whether or not there is force or coercion.'

'As the economic recession hits, many more women are likely to resort to prostitution to feed themselves and their families; if prostitution is forced further underground by these measures the risks they are forced to take will be greater.'
English Collective of Prostitutes – October 2008

* *Scotland has a separate Parliament and legal system and so has different legislation around street prostitution. The Civic Government (Scotland) Act 1982 covers those selling sex in public and the Prostitution (Public Places) (Scotland) Act 2007 covers those buying sex in public. The Policing & Crime Bill will not apply to Scotland.*

⇨ The above information is reprinted with kind permission from politics.co.uk. Visit www.politics.co.uk for more information.
© Adfero

Prostitution: a summary

A briefing from the Fawcett Society

Prostitution in the UK

⇨ An estimated 80,000 people work in prostitution in the UK.

⇨ 9% of men in the UK have paid for sex, and 4.2% have done so in the last five years. In the 1990s, the number of men buying sex in the UK doubled.

⇨ The wider sex industry, including pornography and lap dancing, is expanding and has been shown to have strong links with prostitution, both among women working across the sex industry and clients.

9% of men in the UK have paid for sex

Routes into prostitution

⇨ 52% of women in street prostitution were under 18 when they first worked in prostitution.

⇨ Three-quarters of women in street prostitution report being physically abused by their partners.

⇨ 37% of women in prostitution have spent time in care.

⇨ 22% of women in prostitution were homeless or living in temporary accommodation when they first sold sex.

⇨ 74% of women in indoor prostitution, and 28% of those in street prostitution, cite household expenses and supporting their children financially as their primary motivation.

⇨ 81% of women in off-street prostitution in London are non-UK citizens.

Substance use

⇨ 69% of women working in indoor prostitution, and 93% of women in street prostitution, use illegal drugs.

⇨ 34% of women working in indoor prostitution use significant amounts of alcohol during work hours.

⇨ 62.7% of women working in street

prostitution report that they are doing so to fund an illegal drug habit.

Violence

⇨ 81% of women working in street prostitution and 48% of women in indoor prostitution have experienced client violence.

⇨ A qualitative study found that 27% of women in street prostitution and 8% of women in indoor prostitution reported being raped in the past six months.

⇨ Only one-third of women in prostitution report client violence to the police.

⇨ Reasons for this include concerns about anonymity and disbelief that the criminal justice system will be effective in prosecuting perpetrators.

⇨ 44.1% of street workers compared to 18.6% of indoor workers report violence to the police.

The law

⇨ Street prostitution and loitering or soliciting for prostitution are illegal, as are 'kerb crawling', controlling prostitution for gain and owning or running a brothel.

⇨ In 2003, the Sexual Offences Act set more stringent penalties for people traffickers and those who commercially exploit children.

Current practice

⇨ In 2002, there were 2,678 convictions for soliciting in comparison to only 993 convictions for kerb crawling and 127 for exploitation of prostitution. This means that those working in prostitution were more often punished than their customers or pimps.

⇨ 15 boroughs have no sexual health

outreach provision for women in the sex industry at all.

⇨ Most services currently provided for women in prostitution focus on their sexual health, rather than addressing issues such as prosecuting client violence, housing, drug counselling and education.

⇨ A recent survey found that 82% of support agencies in London identified a lack of provision of safe housing for women wishing to exit prostitution or leave violent pimps.

Alternative policies

⇨ Decriminalisation is designed to improve the working conditions and safety of women in prostitution, by giving them the same rights as other workers. New Zealand has decriminalised prostitution.

⇨ Legalisation brings prostitution under the control of the state and the law. In the Netherlands, for example, brothels must meet conditions regarding their location, management and workplace standards in order to receive a license. This policy has the same aim as decriminalisation but enables greater regulation.

⇨ Criminalising demand is predicated on an understanding of prostitution as a form of gender inequality and male violence against women. Swedish policy accompanied this legal change with funding for prevention, exit strategies and campaigns to change attitudes.

⇨ Criminalisation makes both the buying and selling of sex illegal. This policy is in force throughout most of the USA.

⇨ The above information is reprinted with kind permission from the Fawcett Society. Visit www.fawcettsociety.org.uk for more information and to view references for this piece.

© Fawcett Society

40013159001o

Public's views on prostitution

Information from Ipsos MORI

Ipsos MORI recently undertook a two-part survey for the Government Equalities Office on the subject of prostitution. The first survey, carried out among a representative sample of 1,012 British adults between 11-12 June 2008, found that attitudes towards prostitution are mixed, with almost half (49%) agreeing with the statement 'most prostitutes are only in that role because they are victims of exploitation' and a third (34%) disagreeing. However, almost six in ten (59%) agree with the statement that 'prostitution is a perfectly reasonable choice that women should be free to make', while a quarter (27%) disagree.

The June survey also found that more than a third (37%) say they would not feel ashamed if they found out a family member was working as a prostitute, although 60% say they would feel ashamed. When asked whether they would support or oppose making it illegal to pay for sex as part of an attempt to reduce trafficking of women and children from abroad into prostitution in the UK, almost six in ten (58%) support the measure, while three in ten (31%) oppose it.

The August survey, carried out among a representative sample of 1,010 British adults between 29-31 August 2008, shows that public acceptability of both buying and selling sex drops off when people consider that the buyer or seller is a relation. For example, two in five (39%) feel that it is very or fairly acceptable for a man to purchase sex with a woman, and more than half (52%) find this very or fairly unacceptable. However, when the question asks 'Please imagine that the man purchasing sex is related to you, for example your brother, son or father. In this case would it be acceptable or unacceptable?', acceptability drops 10 points to 29% and unacceptability increases 10 points to 62%.

Similarly, while 38% of the public feel it is acceptable for a woman to sell sex to a man (and 53% find it unacceptable), these figures shift to 22% acceptable and 69% unacceptable when respondents were asked 'to imagine that the woman selling sex is related to you, for example your sister, mother or daughter'.

There is no difference in attitudes towards the legality of purchasing or selling sex: 50% feel the purchase of sex by men should be legal (and 43% think it should be illegal), and 51% feel the sale of sex by women should be legal (and 42% think it should be illegal).

4 September 2008

⇨ The above information is reprinted with kind permission from Ipsos MORI. Visit www.ipsos-mori.com for more information on this and other topics.

© *Ipsos MORI*

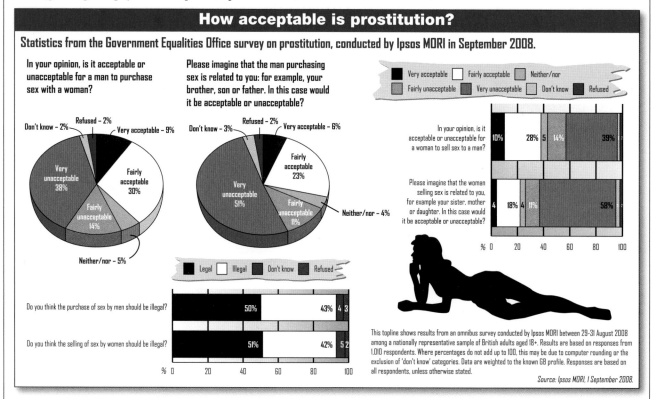

How acceptable is prostitution?

Statistics from the Government Equalities Office survey on prostitution, conducted by Ipsos MORI in September 2008.

In your opinion, is it acceptable or unacceptable for a man to purchase sex with a woman?

- Don't know – 2%
- Refused – 2%
- Very acceptable – 9%
- Fairly acceptable – 30%
- Neither/nor – 5%
- Fairly unacceptable – 14%
- Very unacceptable – 38%

Please imagine that the man purchasing sex is related to you: for example, your brother, son or father. In this case would it be acceptable or unacceptable?

- Don't know – 3%
- Refused – 2%
- Very acceptable – 6%
- Fairly acceptable – 23%
- Neither/nor – 4%
- Fairly unacceptable – 11%
- Very unacceptable – 51%

Legend: Very acceptable | Fairly acceptable | Neither/nor | Fairly unacceptable | Very unacceptable | Don't know | Refused

In your opinion, is it acceptable or unacceptable for a woman to sell sex to a man? — 10% | 28% | 5 | 14% | 39%

Please imagine that the woman selling sex is related to you, for example your sister, mother or daughter. In this case would it be acceptable or unacceptable? — 4 | 18% | 4 | 11% | 58%

Legend: Legal | Illegal | Don't know | Refused

Do you think the purchase of sex by men should be illegal? — 50% | 43% | 4 | 3

Do you think the selling of sex by women should be illegal? — 51% | 42% | 5 | 2

This topline shows results from an omnibus survey conducted by Ipsos MORI between 29-31 August 2008 among a nationally representative sample of British adults aged 18+. Results are based on responses from 1,010 respondents. Where percentages do not add up to 100, this may be due to computer rounding or the exclusion of 'don't know' categories. Data are weighted to the known GB profile. Responses are based on all respondents, unless otherwise stated.

Source: Ipsos MORI, 1 September 2008.

Prostitution – fact or fiction?

Information from the Women's Support Project

Many statements are made about prostitution: about its nature, about the women involved and about how governments should address it. This can often lead to people being misinformed about the reality of prostitution. This article highlights 10 statements commonly made about prostitution and provides additional information to help you distinguish between what is fact and what is fiction.

Women choose to get involved in prostitution

Most women enter prostitution because of lack of choice: it is the men who buy sex who are exercising free choice. It is well documented that the vast majority of women in prostitution are poor, homeless, and have already suffered violence and abuse throughout their life. Many enter prostitution before age 18.

A Glasgow study showed that 24.5% of the women surveyed had entered prostitution before age 18, with 8.2% starting at age 16 or under.

'Where is she tonight? Women, street prostitution and homelessness in Glasgow', by Audrey Stewart, 2000

Prostitution is just sex

The single most harmful aspect of prostitution for women is to have to repeatedly endure unwanted sex. Although the women are agreeing to sexual activity, this is unwanted sexual activity. In order to be able to do it, the women need to learn to dissociate ('split off' in their head). Dissociation can cause lasting psychological harm. Women who are not able to 'split off' will use drugs and/or alcohol to achieve the same effect. This is why women will start to use drugs, or their substance use will rapidly escalate, irrespective of why they first became involved in prostitution.

'I would numb my feelings. I wouldn't even feel like I was in my body. I would actually leave my body and go somewhere else with my thoughts and with my feelings until he got off me and it was over with. I don't know how else to explain it except it felt like rape. It was rape to me.'

Quoted in 'Dissociation Among Women in Prostitution' by Ross, Farley and Schwartz in 'Prostitution, Trafficking and Traumatic Stress' edited by Melissa Farley, 2003. Pg. 206

A Glasgow study showed that 24.5% of the women surveyed had entered prostitution before age 18, with 8.2% starting at age 16 or under

---

Women are in prostitution because they enjoy sex

How much would you need to enjoy sex in order to want to do it 20 or 40 times a day? Apart from the risk of STDs, the human body is not designed for the level of sexual activity that women have to endure in prostitution. It causes physical harm, which has been exacerbated by increased demand for anal intercourse, threesomes and double penetration, which in turn is driven by pornography.

'A girl who enters prostitution at 14 will have submitted to the sexual demands of 4,000 men before she is old enough to drive a car, 8,000 men before she is old enough to vote and 12,000 men before she is deemed mature enough to buy a single beer in many [US] states.'

Vednita Carter & Evelina Giobbe quoted in 'Prostitution, Trafficking and Traumatic Stress' edited by Melissa Farley, 2003. Pg. 277

If it weren't for prostitution, more women and children would be raped

There is absolutely no evidence for this claim. This myth is offensive to men who choose not to abuse and rape women. Does anyone really believe that men are incapable of control, and that they will inevitably rape a woman or child if they are denied sex? In addition, this position ignores the sexual abuse of women in prostitution, which many women who have escaped prostitution refer to as 'bought rape'.

78% of 55 women who sought help from the Council for Prostitution Alternatives in 1991 reported being raped an average of 16 times a year by pimps, and were raped 33 times a year by johns.

Susan Kay Hunter, Council for Prostitution Alternatives Annual Report, 1991, Portland, Oregon, quoted at: http://www.rapeis.org/activism/prostitution/prostitutionfacts.html

It would be better for women if prostitution was legalised and regulated

Prostitution is harmful in and of itself: legalisation doesn't remove that harm – it simply makes the harm legal.

A US survey of 119 women engaged in prostitution reported that performing prostitution was a negative and/or traumatic experience for the women 90% of the time. 52% of the women stated that performing prostitution was physically painful and 76% reported it was emotionally painful. 73% of the women indicated that performing prostitution involved pushing away their true emotions and 70% reported using substances to detach emotionally during prostitution.

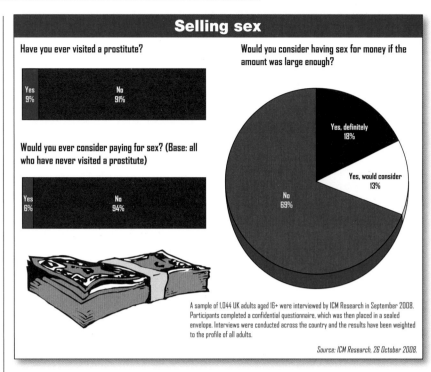

Selling sex

Have you ever visited a prostitute?

Yes 9% No 91%

Would you ever consider paying for sex? (Base: all who have never visited a prostitute)

Yes 6% No 94%

Would you consider having sex for money if the amount was large enough?

Yes, definitely 18%
Yes, would consider 13%
No 69%

A sample of 1,044 UK adults aged 16+ were interviewed by ICM Research in September 2008. Participants completed a confidential questionnaire, which was then placed in a sealed envelope. Interviews were conducted across the country and the results have been weighted to the profile of all adults.

Source: ICM Research, 26 October 2008.

'Emotional Experiences of Performing Prostitution' by Lisa Kramer in 'Prostitution, Trafficking and Traumatic Stress' edited by Melissa Farley, 2003. Pgs. 194–195

Working indoors is safer and offers better conditions for women in prostitution

It doesn't matter where prostitution takes place: unwanted sex is unwanted sex.

In addition to physical violence, women in indoor prostitution report high levels of coercion and control from pimps and brothel owners, including being pressurised or forced not to use condoms, having to see more customers than do women on the street, and having to have sex with pimps or brothel owners, and/or their friends, for free. Women in indoor prostitution also have to compete with each other to be 'picked' by the customer, which causes additional psychological distress.

A report in the *British Medical Journal* about client violence towards women in prostitution stated that of the 125 women in indoor prostitution contacted, 48% had experienced client violence. The types of violence experienced included: slapped, punched, or kicked; robbery; attempted robbery; beaten; threatened with weapon; held against will; attempted rape; strangulation; kidnapped; attempted kidnap; forced to give client oral sex; vaginal rape and anal rape.

'*Violence by clients towards female prostitutes in different work settings: questionnaire survey*' by Stephanie Church et al in BMJ 2001;322:524-525 (3 March)

Legalising or decriminalising prostitution will stop illegal prostitution and trafficking

The legalisation of aspects of prostitution in Australia, and its decriminalisation in New Zealand has resulted in an increase in illegal, hidden and street prostitution. Decriminalisation promotes sex trafficking into countries where prostitution is trivialised. On the other hand it is reported that there has been a dramatic decrease of trafficking into Sweden since that country criminalised the buying of sexual services.

Jonas Trolle, an inspector with the Stockholm police unit dedicated to combating prostitution, said:

'We have significantly less prostitution than our neighbouring countries, even if we take into account the fact that some of it happens underground... We only have between 105 and 130 women – both on the Internet and on the street – active (in prostitution) in Stockholm today. In Oslo, it's 5,000... Another relevant aspect of the ban is the reduction of the number of foreign women now being trafficked into Sweden for sex.

The Swedish government estimates that in the last few years only 200 to 400 women and girls have been annually trafficked into Sweden for prostitution, while in neighbouring Finland the number is 15,000 to 17,000.'

From 'Swedish Prostitution Ban An Apparent Enormous Success' By Thaddeus M. Baklinski, 2007, at http://www.lifesite.net/ldn/2007/nov/07111506.html

If prostitution were legalised and regulated, licensed brothel owners would not hire illegal, underage or trafficked women

Not so. Pimps - owners of brothels, escort agencies and 'saunas'- want to make money. They don't care if someone is illegal, a child or trafficked. Prostitution is a market based on demand and if there is a demand for illegal activity, this will be provided. Pimps, traffickers, procurers and especially punters flock to wherever the prostitution industry is allowed to thrive.

'In New South Wales, brothels were decriminalised in 1995. In 1999, the number of brothels had increased exponentially to 400-500. The vast majority had no license to operate' *Jan Raymond, Coalition Against Trafficking in Women, quoted in 'A Critical Examination of Responses to Prostitution in Four Countries', by Bindel and Kelly, 2004. Pg. 13*

If prostitution were just treated like any other job, this would remove the stigma against the women

As soon as you start to view prostitution as work, the harm is made invisible. Prostitution is intrinsically harmful and traumatic and just calling it a job won't make it harmless. If prostitution were to become just another form of employment, then brothels could advertise in job centres and benefit claimants would risk having their benefit cut if they refused employment in brothels. And how many parents would be happy with the local brothel coming along to the school careers night?

Recognising prostitution as work also means an end to services to support women out of prostitution. If it is 'just a job' why would either the Government or charitable organisations encourage or support women to get out?

'In Germany the service union ver.di offered union membership to Germany's estimated 400,000 sex workers. They would be entitled to health care, legal aid, 30 paid holiday days a year, a five-day workweek and Christmas and holiday bonuses. Out of 400,000 sex workers, only 100 joined the union. That's 0.00025% of German sex workers. Women don't want to be prostitutes.'

'Frequently Asked Questions About Prostitution. 'Answered by S. M. Berg. http://www.oneangrygirl.net/antiporn. html

Legalising prostitution would save a lot of money because police wouldn't have to make arrests, and the state could collect taxes

In every instance where prostitution has been legalised or decriminalised, one of the stated aims has been to reduce crime. Experience has been that you simply get different types of crime, such as gang warfare between different criminal groups, including, for example, firebombing of rival establishments. Brothels shelter other forms of criminality, such as tax evasion. Pimps are simply not going to hand over the massive profits that are a part of the industry. Women in prostitution do not wish to register as a prostitute, nor to pay tax on money earned through unwanted sex.

In addition, decriminalisation has resulted in expensive legal challenges because no one wants prostitution zoned into their neighbourhood or near their children's school, as has happened in New Zealand in the past few years.

'In October 2003 Amsterdam City Council took the decision to close down the street tolerance zone; Mayor Job Cohen noted that the situation was a "devil's dilemma" because 'it appeared impossible to create a safe and controllable zone for women that was not open to abuse by organised crime".'

'A Critical Examination of Responses to Prostitution in Four Countries' by Julie Bindel and Liz Kelly, 2004. Pg. 12

In addition, in 2007 Amsterdam City Council announced it would be closing many of the windows where women are prostituted in the red-light area. Job Cohen stated: 'Since the legalization in 2000, things have changed... The law was created for voluntary prostitution but these days we see trafficking of women, exploitation and all kinds of criminal activity.'
http://www.taipeitimes. com/News/world/ archives/2007/09/22/2003379920

Further information on prostitution can be found at the following websites:

http://womenssupportproject.co.uk: information on the work of the project, including resources available.
http://prostitutionresearch.com: this site offers information and research on women abused through prostitution.
http://catwinternational.org: information on prostitution and trafficking.
http://www.prostitutionrecovery.org: a website to help people escape the life of prostitution, survive and recover from its long-term effects, and to provide education about the effects of prostitution on those used in it, and its effects on the larger community.
http://www.nostatusquo.com/ACLU/ dworkin: a selection of Andrea Dworkin's writing.
http://www.ecpat.org.uk: Website of End Child Prostitution, Child Pornography and the Trafficking of Children for Sexual Purposes.

'A girl who enters prostitution at 14 will have submitted to the sexual demands of 4,000 men before she is old enough to drive a car'

---

http://www.cwasu.org: training, consultancy and research from a feminist perspective.
http://www.myrnabalk.com: website of Myrna Balk, artist and campaigner against sexual exploitation.

⇨ The above information is reprinted with kind permission from the Women's Support Project. Visit www.womenssupportproject.co.uk for more information.
© Women's Support Project

'Callous' sex trafficking gang jailed

By Jon Land

A gang of 'callous' sex traffickers and brothel bosses, who subjected a terrified teenager and a young mother to a nightmare of 'sex slavery', were jailed for up to 14 years each today.

Their youngest victim, a 16-year-old Slovakian, was a virgin when she fell into their clutches.

She sobbed uncontrollably as she described being lured to Britain with promises of a well-paid pub job by one of her mother's so-called friends.

Instead he betrayed her into a seemingly never-ending ordeal of repeated rapes in sleazy brothels, a succession of 'owners', endless customers and frequent violence.

Another victim, a 22-year-old mother, was also snared with empty assurances of well-paid work in London.

She eventually left her baby daughter with relatives in Lithuania, convinced she finally had the opportunity to build a better future for them both.

But the life of luxury painted by one of her brother's old classmates soon saw her in the clutches of a ruthless Albanian gang who forced her to entertain numerous clients.

London's Southwark Crown Court heard during six weeks of degradation and torment she was passed from one group of men to another.

They used and abused her repeatedly, ignoring her pleas for mercy and leaving her pregnant.

The main defendant, Turk Ali Arslan, 43, of Newnton Close, Stamford Hill, north London, admitted two counts of keeping brothels.

The jury trying the case also convicted him of controlling prostitution for gain, controlling a child prostitute and trafficking within the UK for sexual exploitation.

He got 14 years.

His brother-in-law and fellow Turkish national Mesut Arslan, 26, from Harrowgate Road, Upton, east London, was imprisoned for two and a half years after being found guilty of one brothel keeping count and the child prostitution offence.

Slovakian Edward Facuna, 54, of St Mary's Court, Peterborough, and Czech-born Roman Pacan, 39, of nearby Parliament Street, were found guilty of trafficking the teenager into the UK for sexual exploitation and received 11 years each.

Kosovan Martin Doci, 29, of Vale Road, Upton, was also convicted of controlling child prostitution as well as trafficking within the UK for sexual exploitation and was jailed for 11 years.

Albanian Valmir Gjetja, 29, of Avon Road, Greenford, Middlesex, was convicted of controlling prostitution and got three years.

Passing sentence, Judge Martin Beddoe said what happened to the two women was 'despicable and cannot be tolerated in a civilised society.

'In opening the case, prosecution counsel told the jury that slavery was alive and well, and this is what this case has essentially been about.

'Each of you in your various ways was playing a role in a degrading activity producing untold misery.

'Human trafficking, where it exists, exploits the impoverished, the young and the socially disadvantaged.

'Those exploited in such a way by false promises are entitled and deserve the protection of the law and those who engage in their exploitation, whether as traffickers or ending up exploiting the trafficked, must be dealt with and will be dealt with by condign punishment.'

The judge said although the court heard of only two girls being forced to prostitute themselves, Ali

Arslan's brothels employed up to 50 eastern European women and almost certainly included others made to sell their bodies.

But whether willing or not, the 'inescapable conclusion' was all had been trafficked into Britain to help 'line the pockets' of those involved.

However, the teenager's ordeal was particularly disquieting.

She would obviously have been in 'terrible fear of what would happen if she didn't co-operate.

'She was barely able to speak English, was in a strange country, and had no-one to turn to and no-one to trust. And at that stage she had no idea where she actually was.

'What happened to her is a terrible story of betrayal.'

The child was, said the judge, a 'prize' that would help bring her brothel bosses even more money.

'As well as the degradation and misery comes the corruption. It was described during the case as conditioning.

'Because of what the girls like her were made to do she became so despoiled there was no longer pain in doing as she did and she became a willing prostitute, immured to the situation and position to which she had fallen,' said the judge.

He told Ali Arslan his behaviour resulted in the teenager and the older woman becoming 'devastated, humiliated, violated'.

In particular it 'contributed to the misery' of his youngest victim in a 'significant way, scarring her for life.

'You are a callous man and your pretence of compassion I treat as mere humbug. You told a pack of lies.'

The judge added his crimes had enabled him to enjoy a 'fast car' and enjoy London's nightlife with no expense spared.

Opening the six-week case Jeremy Dunn-Shaw said those in the dock 'shared a common greed at the expense of vulnerable women'.

Those unfortunate enough to become their victims had to abide by a list of unbreakable rules, including never arguing with clients and always keeping their room 'neat and tidy'.

But while 'entertaining', they were invariably locked in with customers, and, with no means of escape, were 'often' subjected to vicious beatings.

The teenager, now 18, said she really believed her mother's friend, Facuna, when he told her of the money and happiness awaiting her in Britain.

But after an exhausting road trip across Europe and a ferry to Dover, he and Pacan drove her to Peterborough where she naively believed her pub job beckoned.

Instead, she was handed over to a mystery Albanian man called Claude at the beginning of a 16-month nightmare of pain and degradation that saw her 'broken physically and mentally'.

The youngster said that having groped her 'all over my body', he took her virginity in the first of many rapes and then took her to her first brothel.

Some time later he drove her to Ealing, west London, where he sold her to Doci.

Before putting her to work in a run-down bordello, she was taken shopping for a 'miniskirt, boots, Playboy knickers and make-up' to help titillate clients.

A few weeks and scores of customers later she was sold again, this time for £2,500 to the Arslans, who wanted her for their so-called Mellows Sauna in Luton.

Jurors heard by this stage she was so intimidated that even when allowed out alone she 'felt powerless to run away'.

'She had no means to survive on her own,' explained counsel. 'She knew of no other life in this country and she had no contact with anyone outside of the world she inhabited – pimps, brothels, prostitutes, traffickers and rapists.'

She was then sold to her last 'owner', Gjetja, who once more put her to work as a prostitute.

Even when the teenager plucked up the courage to escape last December, he tracked her down and ordered her to sell her body once more.

Eventually she managed to dial 999 and was finally set free.
4 November 2008

⇨ The above information is reprinted with kind permission from 24dash.com. Visit www.24dash.com for more information.

© *24dash.com*

I'm a sex worker – don't take away my livelihood

The *Big Brothel* report paints women in my industry as victims. Some may be – but to generalise is patronising and offensive

'Sex for £15' and other such findings, including on the availability of unprotected sex, have made the headlines after the release of the *Big Brothel* report, the culmination of the Poppy Project's research into off-street prostitution. Due to the fact that such 'findings' have been reported out of context – for example, only in 2% of cases was unprotected sex on offer, as highlighted in Diane Taylor's brilliant article 'Really lifting the lid?' – all this report has served to do is to paint a very bleak picture of the off-street sex scene which any socially-conscious individual would quite rightfully abhor.

There are many problems with the report, not least the fact that the research was conducted by male researchers posing as prospective clients. Given this, such findings as the average age of the women being 21 have to be taken with a large pinch of salt. It is not unheard of for women in their 30s to be 'advertised' as being 21. At the very least, knocking five years off a woman's age is accepted as an industry standard; thus, adding five years to the woman's advertised age will give a more accurate picture. Furthermore, the report found that 75 different ethnicities were 'on offer'. I don't doubt this is true, but parlours have been known to try to pass off Thai women as Japanese, to give but one example. I would suggest that, knowing the industry as I do, the actual number of women of different ethnicities on offer is somewhat smaller.

Somewhat predictably, the *Big Brothel* report also slams the likes of the ITV2 series *Secret Diary of a Call Girl* as depicting an unrealistic, glamorous off-street sex industry quite removed from the reality. But can a group of male researchers posing as clients, conducting telephone research and not even visiting the brothels in question, really claim to have uncovered the truth about 'what is going on' in the industry?

I am an off-street sex worker. I don't live a Belle de Jour-type existence, but nor am I the trafficked/drug-addled/pimped victim the *Big Brothel* report would have you believe. The reality of my working life lies somewhere between the two.

I feel obliged to state at this point that I have a good degree from a good university, as so many people assume we do this job because we are poor, uneducated souls. I say 'we' because I am not alone – I know many, many women who work the length and breadth of the UK in the same way as I do. I cannot speak for all these women, of course, and I do not intend to try to do so, but suffice it to say that my situation is not an unusual one.

So, what is my situation? I am a single mother with two young children aged four and six. Prior to doing this job – and it is a job – I was employed as a PA in a large, city-based firm. My job was a typical 9-to-5 – which, as everyone who has ever worked in such a job will know, means 7:30am to 6:30pm by the time you take into consideration travelling and (unpaid) overtime. I was dropping my children off at breakfast club at 8am and collecting them at 6pm, by which time we would all be completely knackered. The children go to bed at 7:30pm, meaning we were left with precisely 90 minutes to prepare and eat our evening meal, have baths, get ready for bed and read bedtime stories. It was like we were living in a whirlwind. I felt I never saw my kids – let's face it, I didn't (much) – there was certainly never much time for playing or talking or simply just sitting cuddling on the sofa. The guilt was getting to me. I was unhappy. I hoped they weren't, but I was never sure. Yet, despite the long hours I spent away from home, I was earning just enough to make ends meet. Sure, I could pay the mortgage, but we'd never had a family holiday. By the time my monthly pay packet came around, I would have literally just a few pounds in the bank.

It was by no means a desperate existence – we always had enough food, and the house was always heated – but it was quite empty from my point of view. My children are fantastic human beings and I wanted to spend more time in their company without us suffering financially, it was as simple

as that. I wanted a job which would allow me to work flexible hours to fit around the children's schooling, fewer hours, but without taking the drop in wages which a part-time office job would have led to. Escorting seemed like the natural solution. I say 'natural' because it felt natural to me. I am well aware that this is not a job everybody could do. But as a sexually-aware and sexually-experienced woman in her mid-30s, the thought of having sex with strangers did not terrify me. I remember thinking that I might even enjoy it (and that has proved to be the case).

Promiscuity amongst women is still deemed to be something to be frowned upon

I work from a flat on which I pay the mortgage – I do not have any landlord to worry about. I charge £150 per hour and I get enough enquiries to enable me to choose my own working hours. In a typical day I drop my children off at school at 9am, return home, shower and get changed into my alter-ego, Lara (we never use our own names). I then might have an hour's appointment at 11am and another at 1pm, leaving me with a break of an hour in between to shower and refresh myself. I then fetch myself a late lunch and am at the school again to collect my children at 3:30pm. It works. I never see more than two clients a day; most days I see only one; on other days none at all. Yet in just three hours' work I can earn the same as I used to earn in a week working at the office.

Such is the taboo of sex work, that it is difficult to tell anybody what I do for a living. These taboos are created and exacerbated by reports in the media of all prostitutes being drug addicts and 'dirty'. Promiscuity amongst women is still deemed to be something to be frowned upon. In order to make excuses for our behaviour (because excuses have to be made, of course – no 'normal' woman would choose prostitution for a living) reports such

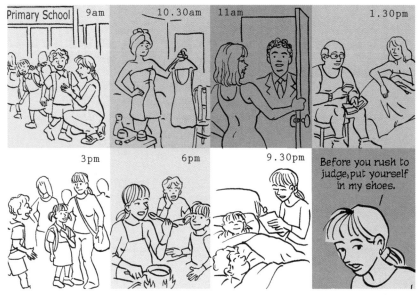

as *Big Brothel* promote the victim status of prostitutes, making such sweeping generalisations such as 'if the women do not have pimps as such, their money will likely go to fund their coping strategies, such as drugs and alcohol'. I find such a statement both patronising and offensive. I do not have a pimp, and nor do I feel the need for 'coping strategies'. I am not *au fait* with drugs and drink only on social occasions. Contrary to what Big Brothel would have you believe, my money pays the mortgage and bills; it pays my income tax and national insurance; it buys food and clothing for my family and, this summer, it paid for the first holiday my children have ever known.

My clients are on the whole middle-aged businessmen. I have never been treated with anything less than respect

by any one of them. I have not been physically or sexually abused by any of them. Of course I have my security systems in place should anything go wrong, but so far nothing has. My children have their mother now, and not just on a part-time basis. I have time with them to enjoy their childhoods, without any of us suffering financially. I am not making big bucks – but I am earning a little more money to boot.

Big Brothel calls for the purchase of sex acts to be criminalised, in order to stem what it calls the 'rise in demand for prostitution' which, it asserts, 'fuels trafficking'. The report does not seem to take into consideration that the type of people who benefit from trafficking, be it for prostitution or otherwise, are likely to pay scant regard to the law; as, indeed, are the men who wish to purchase sex from trafficked

women. Criminalisation would only serve to drive the industry further underground, leaving the women who are victims of trafficking even more vulnerable.

Conversely, making criminals of all men who pay for sex would result in myself and thousands of other women who choose to work in this industry becoming unemployed, and thus instead of contributing to the state (through our taxes) we would be taking from the state in the form of income support, housing benefit and so on. This is how we make a living; it's an industry that prevents many, many women and their children from living on the breadline. If you are going to take our livelihoods from us, the consequences will be devastating.

17 September 2008

Schoolgirls lured into prostitution, warns MP

Schoolgirls as young as 12 are being groomed for prostitution, warns a Labour MP

The grooming of schoolgirls as young as 12 into prostitution by gangs of men is a growing national problem, a senior MP warned today.

Labour's Barry Sheerman, chairman of the Children, Schools and Families Select Committee, claimed skilful methods were being used by criminals to lure teenagers into the sex trade.

He warned the problem was being made worse by the use of the 'sophisticated techniques' and new technology.

He said young men were initially targeting girls at school and acting as their boyfriends before passing them on to older men who would become their pimps.

In a Westminster Hall debate, Mr Sheerman said: 'Children as young as 12 are brought into a life of prostitution.

'In every town and city there are unscrupulous men who have a very sophisticated methodology and technique of grooming children.

'It is a problem and it is getting worse in a very real way.'

The MP said he knew of cases in his Huddersfield constituency where girls first met young men, perhaps driving 'flash cars' outside school, who made the initial contact.

They then took them out and introduced them to drink and drugs before embarking on a sexual relationship.

The girl would believe they were with their first boyfriend but before long, older men would take over,

forcing them to have sex and selling them to others.

He likened the psychological techniques employed at first to those used by US cult leaders. He added: 'These men who prey on children have great skill in identifying the vulnerability of these children whatever the background they come from.'

He added: 'It is getting worse because of the technology. Children are more vulnerable through the Internet and through mobile phones.'

Mr Sheerman said there was evidence that where multi-agency approaches were used between police and child services the problem could be curtailed.

He said: 'I believe the grooming of a child, whether it is by the teacher in the classroom, on the Internet or grooming by a man in a flash car outside the school they are groomers. I don't like them, I believe they are criminals and they should be treated as such.'

Junior Home Office minister Alan Campbell said the Government took the issue of child prostitution and exploitation 'very seriously'.

He said: 'The safeguarding of children is an absolute priority and the exploitation of children is entirely unacceptable.

'Whatever community it occurs in and whatever community it comes from it is simply wrong.'

He said that in relation to Huddersfield, a 'number of police operations' were ongoing and he could

not go into detail for fear of harming any future prosecutions.

The Government had issued guidance around the protection of children and more would follow later this year.

He added: 'It is important that we have sophisticated responses to this.

'We are very concerned...about the issue of trafficking because it is a form of trafficking within the borders of the UK.

'Often it is teenage girls who are targeted for exploitation and then trafficked between and indeed within towns and cities and this is entirely unacceptable. The Government is committed to tackling this problem.'
20 January 2009

⇨ The above information is reprinted with permission from 24-dash.com. Visit www.24dash.com for more.
© *24-dash.com*

International approaches to prostitution

An extract from the CARE document *Tackling the demand for prostitution and sex trafficking*

Various legislative approaches to managing prostitution have been employed abroad. This article examines the approaches in New Zealand, the Netherlands, Australia, Germany, Finland and Sweden and how the legislation has impacted individuals involved in the sex industry.

New Zealand

In 2003 New Zealand introduced the Prostitution Reform Act which decriminalised prostitution.

In February 2004 the New Zealand Prostitution Reform Act Sub-Committee met to discuss the problems that had persisted since the change in legislation. The health and safety of the individuals in street prostitution was still at a low level and had not been improved by the Act's implementation. Perceived threats to passers-by, hazardous litter left in public places and alleged undertaking of sexual activities in public places and adjacent property were still an unresolved issue.

Streetreach, an Auckland-based project that helps individuals involved in the sex industry, stated that before decriminalisation they would make contact with 30 clients a night, and are now coming into regular contact with 90 clients a night. Streetreach has also noticed that there has been

a rise in drug use and an increase in gang involvement in 'minding' the sex workers. Debbie Baker, Director of Streetreach, recently disclosed to CARE that the women they are in contact with have experienced an increase in physical and sexual violence, such as rape, since 2003.

A report by the Manukau City Council indicates that the number of street workers in Manukau City may have quadrupled since June 2003. Police in Auckland and Christchurch believe that the number of street workers has increased since the passing of the PRA and that the number of underage girls has increased. The New Zealand Collective of Prostitutes has admitted that the numbers of individuals involved has not decreased in Wellington and has in fact increased in Christchurch.

The Government hoped that the introduction of the legislation would result in an increase of women choosing to work from their own homes. Research collected one year on

showed that this had not happened.

There has also been a perceived increase in the number of children involved in prostitution since the legislation was introduced. Mama Tere, a woman who used to be in prostitution, told New Zealand Newspaper *Morning Report* that the Prostitution Reform Act has normalised behaviour and youth gangs are now pimping their members. Streetreach have also made contact with a significant number of children in prostitution. In 2007 the US Department of State made the observation that child trafficking and prostitution is now a major problem in New Zealand.

The Netherlands

Prostitution was legalised in the Netherlands in 2000 in order to regulate the sex industry and bring the associated criminal activity under control. However, over the last decade the sex industry in the Netherlands has expanded by 25% and now accounts for 5% of the economy. In November 2003 a Bill to combat smuggling and trafficking in human beings was introduced into legislation and later amended in January 2005.

Experts estimate that as many as two-thirds of the women working in prostitution are foreigners. The

Amsterdam-based ChildRight organisation estimates that at least 5,000 of the children in prostitution are from other countries, with a large segment being Nigerian girls.

Dutch NGOs report that most of the foreign women working in prostitution have been trafficked into the country since it is almost impossible for poor women to facilitate their own migration, underwrite the costs of travel and travel documents, and set themselves up in 'business' without outside help.

Femke Halsema, a member of the Dutch Parliament who advocated the measure, recently said: 'I have often doubted, since we legalised the brothels, whether we did the right thing. For me, it was a question of emancipation and liberation for the women, but for now it is working the other way.'

In 2005 the Dutch police received more than 600 reports of women who may have been forced in prostitution and 400 women contacted anti-trafficking organisations for assistance. Although laws against sex trafficking are in place, acceptance of the sex industry through legalisation has actually witnessed an increase in forced prostitution, the grooming of young girls and abusive situations for many vulnerable women. In 2005, Mayor of Amsterdam, Job Cohen, stated: 'Almost five years after the lifting of the brothel ban, we have to acknowledge that the aims of the law have not been reached. Lately, we've received more and more signals that abuse still continues. The police admit we are in the midst of modern slavery.'

Australia

The Australian state of Victoria legalised brothel and escort prostitution in 1984. Since then several other states have legalised or decriminalised brothel prostitution. Among the main arguments given in favour of legalisation/decriminalisation were that it would limit the growth of the sex industry, end organised crime involvement, reduce police corruption and reduce violence experienced by the women and girls in prostitution. None of these, however, have materialised.

In Sydney the number of brothels tripled to over 400 between 1995, when they were decriminalised, and 1999, with many of these having no licence to operate.

Violence is still a common experience for those working in the trade. The brothel The Daily Planet in Melbourne, which is listed on the Australian stock exchange, has alarm buttons in every room. According to one bouncer who works there, the use of these buttons – after the woman has been hit or assaulted – is not uncommon.

Trafficked women are sold to both legal and illegal brothels in Victoria. Traffickers make it possible for the women to work in legal brothels by applying for refugee status on their behalf. It is estimated that $1 million is earned from trafficked women weekly.

Germany

Germany legalised prostitution in 2003. The subsequent effects of the legislation have been concerning. Several German NGOs now estimate that as many as 75% of women in brothels are from abroad. In 2005 one German woman was told by her local jobcentre that her employment benefits would be cut if she refused to work in prostitution. As a result of legalisation, the industry is forcing vulnerable people into prostitution.

Finland

It is estimated that a third of all individuals in prostitution in Finland come from abroad and are controlled by pimps. In June 2006 Finland's Parliament enacted into law a Bill which made the act of purchasing sexual services a crime in circumstances involving procuring or trade in human beings. Although this is an offence which should be criminalised, legislation which is limited only to trafficking victims poses some challenges.

There is no explicit mention in Finnish legislation that the buyer must have had knowledge that trafficking took place in order to be prosecuted. However, in practice the police have to prove that the buyer had knowledge that the individual was a victim of trafficking in order to secure a conviction. This has presented a challenge to the authorities in implementing the law.

Sweden

In January 1999, the Swedish Government introduced a law that made purchasing – or attempting to purchase – sexual services a criminal offence, punishable by a six-month fine or imprisonment.

The key policy principle in Sweden is that 'prostitution is regarded as an aspect of male violence against women and children' and that prostitution is a problem causing harm to society. This leads to an abolitionist model of 'zero tolerance', based on a gender-equality policy emphasising the relationships between men and women. The aim is that 'the law and its enforcement have an overall preventative effect that will make the clients and the basis for the market disappear.'

The legislative change has led to a much needed discussion regarding the root causes of prostitution and trafficking in women resulting in a changing attitude towards the acceptance of purchasing sexual services. During the 2006 World Cup in Germany, a team of researchers carried out a survey asking men of different nationalities about their opinions on buying sex. In contrast to many of the men questioned, not a single Swede said that engaging in prostitution was acceptable. This demonstrates the extent to which the Swedish legislation, along with accompanying measures, has reduced the demand for paid sex among Swedish men.

The Swedish government states that there has been a 'dramatic drop' in the number of individuals in street prostitution and the number of men buying services. The National Criminal Intelligence Service acts as the Swedish National Rapporteur on trafficking in human beings and annually compiles and analyses information on the scale of trafficking in Sweden and between other countries. Ekberg quotes the 2003 and 2004 reports that the Law on Purchasing Sexual Services has 'had positive effects in limiting the trafficking of women into Sweden' and compares the numbers with those from other Baltic countries. The 2005 report also makes a similar observation, quoting the hundreds of Nigerians on the streets of Oslo, saying 'so far the legislation relating to purchase of sexual services seems to constitute an effective obstacle.'

One of the objectives of the legislation was that it would create an incentive for women involved in prostitution to leave. NGOs believe the legislation has been a success, with more people seeking help to leave prostitution and acting as a deterrent to women who previously had the type of background which led to prostitution, including prostitution in brothels, lap dancing clubs and through escort agencies.

This approach has reduced the profitability of human trafficking into Sweden. As previously stated, the trafficking and pimping of people is a highly lucrative business. When the market is reduced, there is less money to be made and less reason to engage in the activity.
June 2008

⇨ The above information is an extract from the document *Tackling the demand for prostitution and sex trafficking*, and is reprinted with kind permission from CARE. Visit www.care.org.uk to view the full text and references.

© CARE

New prostitution laws 'unenforceable'

Information from politics.co.uk

The government's new prostitution proposals have been criticised as unenforceable by the UK's head of anti-trafficking.

The new measures, announced last month by home secretary Jacqui Smith, would mean that men would be breaking the law if they paid for sex with a woman trafficked into the UK or working for a pimp, regardless of whether the man was aware the woman was forced into prostitution.

Commander Allan Gibson, head of the Met's anti-trafficking unit, said to the Commons home affairs committee: 'Speaking personally, I think that is going to be very difficult to enforce.'

Men would be breaking the law if they paid for sex with a woman trafficked into the UK or working for a pimp

Committee chairman Keith Vaz told minister for women Harriet Harman: '[Commander Gibson] says it is very difficult to enforce a situation where a man is expected to ask a prostitute whether or not she has been trafficked and even if he gets a negative answer he is still to be prosecuted.

'The police themselves... feel that the new proposals are unenforceable.'

That sentiment has been echoed by Chris Huhne, Liberal Democrat home affairs spokesman, who said the new measures will force these vulnerable women further underground.

Mr Huhne said: 'The Finnish system of criminalising the clients of exploited and trafficked women is a bad model. It has had a poor record of successful prosecutions, precisely because the women deny a problem and juries are reluctant to convict when the client says they were misled.

'The government's other proposals run the risk of driving already vulnerable women underground and into the hands of pimps and pushers.'

The new measures are based on the laws currently operating in Finland, which have been in place since 2006.
10 December 2008

⇨ The above information is reprinted with kind permission from politics.co.uk. Visit www.politics.co.uk for more information.

© Adfero

New measures to penalise men who pay for sex with exploited women have been branded 'unenforceable' by critics

New laws will make sex workers more vulnerable

By Catherine Stephens of the International Union of Sex Workers

Yesterday the Home Office announced new proposals intended to 'protect the thousands of vulnerable women coerced, exploited or trafficked into prostitution in our country, and to bring those who take advantage of them to justice'. It's a great story, with drama, heroism, anguish and a big white horse for Jacqui Smith to ride as she swoops in to rescue tearful hookers from foreign countries.

Unfortunately, it's pretty much fact-free and bears no relationship to the reality of the sex industry: it will in actuality increase the vulnerability of all women who sell sex, even privileged, educated, white, British-passport-holding women like me. How come?

If you want to target trafficking, the first thing you need to do is increase reporting. You can't rely on police raids to find the real victims – who do exist – in the sex industry. Pentameter 1, raiding 515 premises, found 88 victims of trafficking. This spectacularly fails to match the Turkish hotline for reporting anxieties about trafficking (in any field: hotel and catering, domestic service, agriculture...). Three-quarters of the tip-offs came from sex workers' clients, and those calls resulted in the destruction of 10 trafficking networks and freedom of 100 women from coercion. And I bet that didn't cost the £5 million reported cost of Pentameter 1.

And speaking of agriculture, to put trafficking for sexual exploitation in perspective, Pentameter's 88 rescues over seven months compares with 60 suspected trafficked labourers found in one day, on one farm in Lincolnshire.

Clients do not want to pay for sex with women who are not willing. Even the Poppy Project, which campaigns for their criminalisation (and considers 'Kissing available for £20 "depending on what you look like"' to be an anecdotal indicator of trafficking (*Big Brothel*, p23)) receive 2% of their referral from clients, and a further 6% from unspecified 'members of the public'. Further Poppy research shows that 2% of clients would stop paying for sex if it were criminalised – this is, by definition, the most law-abiding, conscientious type of client, least likely to harm and most likely to report anxieties. If 98% will not stop, it is clear that the industry will be pushed further underground.

Clients do not want to pay for sex with women who are not willing

---

Yet will implicating yourself in a crime – that you are guilty of even if you didn't know you were committing it at the time, according to some reports of how the Home Office plan to structure new laws – increase reporting? I don't think so.

British law already endangers sex workers by making it illegal for us to work together; criminal gangs know this, and knowingly target sex workers for robbery and rape. Brothel keepers who have reported fears they've been offered trafficked women – that have been proven true, with victims rescued and traffickers imprisoned – have themselves been prosecuted, imprisoned, and their assets seized as a result of coming to the attention of the authorities.

In nearly ten years in the sex industry I have never met someone who believes they have the full protection of the law. Increasing the criminalisation of our industry, and of our clients, will help no-one and harm many.

Only inclusion within the law of people in the sex industry will produce real, effective, long-lasting, positive change. The government had a chance to create this, but has opted to perpetuate social exclusion, whilst bewailing its consequences.

About Catherine Stephens

After a string of jobs in the private sector, including estate agency, television and administration for an architectural practice, Catherine spent ten years with an environmental campaigning organisation and a further five working with community development organisations. For the past eight years she has worked in the sex industry, and has been involved in sex worker organising for most of that time. She is an activist with the International Union of Sex Workers and is a member of the GMB trades union's branch for people who work in the sex industry. She loves her job.

20 November 2008

⇨ This article was originally published in the independent online magazine www.opendemocracy.net

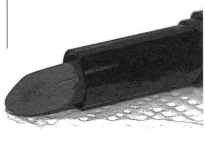

Human trafficking and the sex industry

The problem today

Lea Kna, from Cambodia, was sold at the age of six by her parents who lived in poverty. The buyer, a family friend, transported her across the border into Thailand where she was re-sold to a brothel and forced into child prostitution.

Anna, 15, arrived in Heathrow airport thinking she would be spending her summer holiday baby-sitting in London to earn some extra pocket money. The man who met her took her to a coffee shop in the airport where he sold her to a brothel owner for £3000. Forced into prostitution, Anna was told that if she tried to escape, her family back home in Russia would be harmed.

Every year men, women and children are bought and sold. Often traffickers will use threats, manipulation and debt bondage to ensure that their victims do not escape. CARE is focussing on the plight of women, children and men trafficked into prostitution in the UK and across the world. Many are kept in appalling conditions and are forced to see dozens of clients a day. Research shows that those who are rescued often share similar symptoms with survivors of torture.

The CARE campaign focuses on three areas: demand, victim support and education.

Demand

Trafficking for the purpose of sexual exploitation is currently a high-profit, low-risk venture for those who trade in people. It has been reported that some drug trafficking gangs have switched to people trafficking as there is more money to be made and less risk of being caught. The number of British people buying sexual services has more than doubled in a recent ten-year period, fuelling demand for prostitution. There is a ready-made market for pimps, gangs and traffickers to exploit and make high levels of profit.

Although kerb crawling in England and Wales has been an offence since 1985, at present there is no deterrent in the law to deal with demand in an off-street context. Until the root cause is addressed, a significant reduction in sex trafficking and other forms of prostitution will not be realised.

CARE is campaigning for the demand for sex trafficking and prostitution to be sufficiently tackled, therefore bringing a reduction in the number of people recruited and exploited in this way.

Victim support

It is vital that adequate care and protection is given to survivors of trafficking. Survivors are often extremely traumatised and need medical and psychological assistance as well as support for re-integration into society.

Although rescued from the exploitative situation, trafficked individuals are often still very vulnerable to being found and re-sold by their traffickers. It is therefore vital that they are looked after in a safe environment.

Trafficking for the purpose of sexual exploitation is currently a high-profit, low-risk venture for those who trade in people

---

Due to the intimidation that individuals face from their traffickers and pimps, victims can often be hesitant to share their stories with the police and immigration staff. Unfortunately this can lead to cases of trafficking victims ending up in UK detention centres and being exported back to source countries where they may face violence and re-trafficking.

NGOs across Europe are working hard to make help and assistance more easily accessible to victims of trafficking. CARE's office in Brussels has been working with Stop the Traffik and Oasis Trust in promoting an EU Written Declaration calling for a single European helpline number for victims of trafficking as well as

provision in the EU budget for this to be serviced by suitable NGOs. The budget has now been approved and the EU Commission has called for a tender to realise the feasibility study which will start this summer.

Council of Europe Convention

The UK has now signed and ratified the Council of Europe Convention on Action against Trafficking in Human Beings. The Convention will come into force on 1 April 2009. CARE was among several NGOs who campaigned for the UK Government to sign the Convention.

The Convention gives provision for the care and protection of survivors of trafficking, including a reflection period where an individual will receive safe housing, medical care and assistance. The UK Government has committed to providing a 45-day recovery period, which is to be commended. However, due to the

health and trauma consequences of trafficking, a minimum of 90 days is preferable.

CARE works in partnership with Beyond the Streets which exists to unite, equip and empower groups working with people involved in prostitution to offer freedom and change. Beyond the Streets has over 45 affiliated projects who work with around 4,000 people caught up in prostitution throughout the UK.

Education

In order to reduce trafficking in the UK it is vital that people are aware that it is happening and know how to spot the signs. Police, BIA staff, social workers, teachers and healthcare staff may come across victims of trafficking. However, it is not just members of the above professions who may come into contact with trafficking situations. People are trafficked into towns and

cities all over the UK. There may be trafficked people being held on your street.

If you suspect a case of trafficking, contact Crimestoppers on 0800 555 111.

CARE recognises that it is especially important to educate potential victims of the dangers of trafficking, especially in countries of origin. There is also a need to educate children in the UK of the dangers of being groomed for prostitution and trafficked internally by criminal gangs.

There is also a need to educate buyers and potential buyers of sexual services of the reality of the sex trade.

⇨ The above information is reprinted with kind permission from CARE. Visit www.care.org.uk for more information.

© CARE

The myth of trafficking

Most migrant women, including those in the sex industry, have made a clear decision, says a new study, to leave home and take their chances abroad. They are not 'passive victims' in need of 'saving' or sending back by western campaigners

Brendan O'Neill reviews Sex at the Margins: Migration, Labour Markets and the Rescue Industry by Laura María Agustín (Zed Books, 224pp, £16.99).

It is always refreshing to read a book that turns an issue on its head. Laura María Agustín's trenchant and controversial critique of the anti-trafficking crusade goes a step further: it lays out the matter – in this case, 'human trafficking' – on the operating table, dissects it, unravels its innards, and shows the reader, in gory, sometimes eye-watering detail, why everything we think about it is Wrong with a capital W. It's a jarring read; I imagine that those who make a living from campaigning against the scourge of human trafficking will throw it violently across the room, if not into an incinerator. Yet it may also be one of the most important books on migration published in recent years.

Most of us recognise the ideological underpinnings of old-style baiting of migrants. When newspaper hacks or

By Brendan O'Neill

populist politicians talk about evil Johnny Foreigners coming here and stealing our jobs or eating our swans, it does not take much effort to sniff out their xenophobic leanings. Agustín's contention is that the new 'discourse' on migrants (in which many of them, especially the women and children, are seen as 'victims of trafficking' in need of rescue) is also built on ideological foundations. Like its demented cousin – tabloid hysteria about foreign scroungers – the trafficking scare is based on a deeply patronising view of migrants, rather than any hard statistical evidence that human trafficking is rife.

Agustín begins by challenging the idea that there is a 'new slave trade' in which hundreds of thousands of women and children are sold like chattels across borders. The US state department claims that between

600,000 and 800,000 people are trafficked for forced labour or sex worldwide every year; Unicef says a million children and young people are trafficked each year. Upmarket newspapers – which have embraced the seemingly PC 'trafficking discourse' with the same fervour as the tabloid newspapers

screech about fence-leaping job-stealers from Sangatte – tell us that 'thousands' of women and children have been trafficked into Britain and 'traded for tawdry sex', and that some of them (the African ones) 'live under fear of voodoo'.

The trafficking scare is based on a deeply patronising view of migrants, rather than any hard statistical evidence that human trafficking is rife

---

Agustín says the numbers are 'mostly fantasies'. She does not doubt that there are instances of forced migration, or that, in a world where freedom of movement is restricted by stiff laws and stringent border controls, many aspiring migrants have little choice but to seek assistance from dodgy middlemen. Yet, having researched trafficking and sex workers' experiences for the past five years, both academically and through fieldwork in Latin America and Asia, she concludes that the figures are based on 'sweeping generalisations' and frequently on 'wild speculation'. 'Most of the writing and activism [on trafficking] does not seem to be based on empirical research, even when produced by academics,' she notes. Many of the authors rely on 'media reports' and 'statistics published with little explanation of methodology or clarity about definitions'.

Agustín points out that some anti-trafficking activists depend on numbers produced by the CIA (not normally considered a reliable or neutral font of information when it comes to international issues), even though the CIA refuses to 'divulge its research methods'. The reason why the 'new slavery' statistics are so high is, in part, that the category of trafficking is promiscuously defined, sometimes disingenuously so. Some researchers automatically label migrant women who work as prostitutes 'trafficked persons', basing their rationale on the notion that no woman could seriously want to work in the sex industry. The Coalition Against Trafficking in Women argues that 'all children and the majority of women in the sex trade' should be considered 'victims of trafficking'. As Agustín says, such an approach 'infantilises' migrant women, 'eliminating any notion that women who sell sex can consent'. Ironically, it objectifies them, treating them as unthinking things that are moved around the world against their will.

The reality is very different, the author says. Most migrant women, including those who end up in the sex industry, have made a clear decision to leave home and take their chances overseas. They are not 'passive victims' who must be 'saved' by anti-trafficking campaigners and returned to their country of origin. Rather, frequently, they are headstrong and ambitious women who migrate in order to escape 'small-town prejudices, dead-end jobs, dangerous streets and suffocating families'. Shocking as it might seem to the feminist social workers, caring police people and campaigning journalists who make up what Agustín refers to as the 'rescue industry', she has discovered that some poor migrant women 'like the idea of being found beautiful or exotic abroad, exciting desire in others'. I told you it was controversial.

One of Agustín's chief concerns is that the anti-trafficking crusade is restricting international freedom of movement. What presents itself as a campaign to protect migrants from harm is actually making their efforts to flee home, to find work, to make the most of their lives in often difficult and unforgiving circumstances, that much harder. She writes about the 'rescue raids' carried out by police and non-governmental organisations, in which even women who vociferously deny having been trafficked may be arrested, imprisoned in detention centres and sent back home – for the benefit of their own mental stability, of course. It used to be called repatriation; now, dolled up in therapeutic lingo, it is called 'rescue'.

For all its poisonous prejudices, the old racist view of migrants as portents of crime and social instability at least treated them as autonomous, sentient, albeit 'morally depraved', adults. By contrast, as the author illustrates, the anti-trafficking lobby robs migrants of agency and their individual differences, and views them as a helpless, swaying mass of thousands who must be saved by the more savvy and intelligent women of the west and by western authorities.

Agustín reserves her most cutting comments for the flourishing 'rescue industry', arguing convincingly that it is driven by a colonial-style, maternalistic attitude to foreign women. In its world, 'victims become passive receptacles and mute sufferers who must be saved, and helpers become saviours – a colonialist operation'. Bitingly, she compares today's anti-trafficking feminists with the 'bourgeois women' of the 19th century who considered it a moral virtue to save poor prostitutes, who were 'mistaken, misled, deviant'. Like them, anti-trafficking crusaders see women as weak, easily victimised, and in need of guidance from a caring chaperone.

In truth, poor women – and men and children – migrate for many different reasons and have many different experiences, some good, some bad, some tragic. Such migrants are wise and wily, says Agustín; they have gumption, ambition and hope; they are often cosmopolitan, too, working, mixing and having flings with migrants from the other side of the world whom they meet in some big city in Europe or the United States. And many of them have far more liberal attitudes to freedom of movement than the westerners who campaign on their behalf. She quotes a Kurdish migrant to the Netherlands who thinks borders should be abolished: 'I don't come from the sun or moon. I'm from earth just like everybody else and the earth belongs to all of us.' Now that's an argument I can get behind.

Brendan O'Neill is the editor of 'spiked'
(www.spiked-online.com).
27 March 2008

⇨ The above information is reprinted with kind permission from the *New Statesman*. Visit www.newstatesman.com for more information.

© *New Statesman*

Pornography

Information from Eaves

Introduction and background

⇨ In 1874, 130,000 photos of pornography were discovered in a police raid in London.[1] One century later, Victorian censorship was relaxed and restrictions on pornography were lifted. Hardcore pornography was not yet legal in the UK, but softcore magazines were sold under the counter in concealed packaging.

⇨ The cultural and sexual revolution of the 1960s and 1970s, rather than liberating all women from male subjugation, facilitated an explosion in commercial sexual exploitation on an unprecedented scale.

⇨ It has been known for decades that the pornography industry is responsible for driving the development of viewing technology. The introduction of home videos in the 1970s precipitated the demise of the 'dirty mac brigade'[2] and advanced the proliferation of pornography, from VHS to DVD, then onto the Internet and live streaming on mobile devices.

⇨ Pornography enjoys the biggest profit margin of any medium, raking in at least $57bn worldwide annually[3] (the UK slice accounts for more than £1bn), attracting more than 68mn daily search engine requests and exposing an estimated 80% of 15- to 17-year-olds to hardcore images.[4]

⇨ The effect of the prevalence of pornography is not 'harmless' as its millionaire producers might try to suggest, but rather 'reinforces and normalizes sexual disorders'[5] and thus plays a key role in fostering demand for sexually exploitative encounters in the real world.

⇨ Pathological 'pornography distortion' can occur rapidly, especially among teenagers. A study in the US exposed college undergraduates in three groups to varying levels of pornography over six weeks. At the end of the study their attitudes towards women and sexual violence were measured. The group exposed to the most pornography in that period – just five hours of videos over six weeks – believed that 'rapists deserved milder punishments, that women's liberation was not a good idea [and] they became more callous toward women',[6] significantly more than the groups which had watched less pornography.

Sexualised images of women exist across all media

⇨ Highly sexualised images of young women and girls exist across all media, including mainstream television and public advertising. They are routinely presented as expressions of sexual liberation, rather than exploitation. The commodification of women and girls, which is central to the majority of pornographic material, fuels demand for commercial sex acts, which in turn increases sex trafficking.[7]

⇨ Recent years have seen a rise in the popularity of 'torture porn' films[8] – mainstream blockbusters offering extreme pornographic violence, almost exclusively inflicted upon young women and girls.

Facts and figures

⇨ The UK porn industry is estimated to be worth about £1bn, compared with £20 billion worldwide.

⇨ Almost 40% of the male population used pornographic websites in 2005.[9] British Internet users search for 'porn' online more than anyone else in the English-speaking world.

⇨ Half of UK children (7mn) have encountered pornography on the Internet 'while looking for something else'.[10] A survey of 1,000 teenage girls in 2005 found that 63% of schoolgirls want to be glamour models.

⇨ In January 2008, a BBC survey found that three-quarters of therapists said excessive use of Internet pornography was the most common cause of sex addiction.

⇨ In 2004, 'lads' mags' *Nuts* and *Zoo* launched, competing in a ratings war which included weekly nipple counts and increasingly pornographic images of women in order to boost sales.

UK law and policy

⇨ Hardcore pornography was legalised in the UK in 2000, decades after many other European states.

⇨ Legislation includes the Obscene Publications Acts 1959/1964, Indecent Displays Control Act 1981, Video Recordings Act 1984 and the Criminal Justice & Immigration Act 2008.

⇨ In 2006, the Sexually Explicit Material (Regulation of Sale and Display) Bill failed to gain a second reading; legally, lads' mags are available on any shelf, without protective packaging, despite guidelines.

⇨ In December 2008, *Top Shelf Report*

published findings that 100% of sixth form girls surveyed were angry, upset or offended by images of women in *Nuts*, *Zoo* and the *Daily Sport*, compared to only 11% of sixth form boys, although one-fifth of male respondents thought such pictures encouraged them to view women as objects.

In 2008, the Criminal Justice & Immigration Act introduced the term 'extreme pornography' (Part 5, section 63-68) to cover sexual images which (a) threaten human life; (b) cause serious injury to sexual body parts; (c) involve human corpses; or (d) involve animals – or appear to do so.

Policy dispute is centred on ensuring protection for those who suffer harm and exploitation through pornography without infringing the civil liberties of those who enjoy or profit from it.

Eaves' view

⇨ Pornography is routinely used as a control mechanism for women exploited in the sex industry.

⇨ In this digital age, children may receive their earliest sex 'education' from hardcore pornography, viewed online either accidentally or intentionally. The effects of such early exposure are as yet unknown, but seem unlikely to lead to happy, healthy sex lives for all.

FAQs

Isn't watching porn just harmless fun?
Various studies on prolonged consumption of pornography have found a range of sociopathic effects including violence, desensitisation, sexual dysfunction, social exclusion, exploitative behaviour and paedophilia.[11] Convictions for child pornography offences quadrupled between 2002 and 2004 (Home Office, 2005).

Does 'DIY porn' count as grassroots activism?[12]
Some argue that DIY porn is positive because it shows real people having real sex, thereby undermining the glossy machine of professional porn. However, there is no way to verify the ages or consent of people involved, not to mention violations of privacy or copyright issues.

Doesn't porn prevent sex attacks?
There is a growing case file of assaults where the perpetrator watched large amounts of violent pornography before committing attacks.[13] The rise of the Internet has served to link up paedophiles across the globe through online communities, offering validation through normalisation.

100% of sixth form girls surveyed were angry, upset or offended by images of women in *Nuts*, *Zoo* and the *Daily Sport*, compared to only 11% of sixth form boys

---

What you can do

⇨ Volunteer and/or donate to organisations which campaign against exploitation through pornography, such as the Lilith Project (www.eaves4women.co.uk) and Object (www.object.org.uk/TakeAction).

⇨ Write to your local MP calling for independent and socially responsible monitoring of the UK pornography industry, including adult online exploitation.

⇨ Campaign and complain in your local shops about the display of lads mags and insist that such titles are relocated to the top shelf, if not removed altogether.[14]

Notes

1 Dines, G. (1997). *Pornography: The Production and Consumption of Inequality*. UK: Routledge.

2 A term used to describe men who frequented Soho's adult cinemas, so called for their habit of wearing long mackintosh coats in order to masturbate discreetly in movie theatres.

3 Of which $3 billion is generated through child pornography alone.

4 Internet Pornography Statistics, Jerry Ropelato, TopTenREVIEWS 2007. http://internet-filterreview.toptenreviews.com/internet-pornography-statistics.html Published 24 October 2006

5 Dr. Robert Weiss, Sexual Recovery Institute, *Washington Times*, 26 January 2000

6 Mary Anne Layden, PhD. 'Testimony for US Senate Committee on Commerce, Science & Transportation' (1999).

7 For discussion of the intersection between prostitution and pornography, refer to 'Prostitution Online' by Donna M. Hughes, published in *Prostitution, Trafficking and Traumatic Stress* (2003).

8 Also known as 'gorno.' Examples include *Hostel 1 and 2* (2005 and 2007, dir. Eli Roth); *Grindhouse 1 and 2* (2007 and 2008, dir. Quentin Tarantino).

9 Nielsen NetRatings for *Independent on Sunday*, 2006.

10 Buckingham, D. & Gragg, S. (2003). *Young People, Media and Personal Relationships*. London: Institute of Education.

11 E.g. Zillmann, D. (1989). 'Effects of Prolonged Consumption of Pornography in Pornography: Research Advances and Policy Considerations.' New Jersey: Lawrence Erlbaum Associates. Also, Layden, M.A. (1999).

12 Homemade pornography has leapt in popularity since the advent of low-price video cameras and 3G mobile devices. YouPorn, a video-sharing website, launched in August 2006 was the most popular and largest pornographic website online by October 2007.

13 For one example, the case of Graham Coutts, who killed Jane Longhurst in 2003, following years of consuming necrophilic pornography, preceded by thoughts of murdering women since the age of 15.

14 For information and advice on porn-free shops: http://www.hamdyspornfree.com/Menu.html

December 2008

⇨ The above information is reprinted with kind permission from Eaves. Visit www.eaves4women.co.uk for more information.

© *Eaves*

The law and pornography

Information from CARE

There is no legal definition of pornography, which is very confusing! Below is a simple explanation of what the law means in most of the situations you will come across. The law applies to the Internet in the same way as it would apply to any other type of media. What is illegal offline is illegal online.

Here are some frequently asked questions:

The Criminal Justice and Immigration Act 2008 has introduced a new offence of being in possession of 'extreme pornographic material'

How old do I have to be to buy a top shelf magazine?

Strictly speaking, legally-acceptable pornographic magazines displayed on the top shelf of a newsagent can be sold legally to anyone of any age. They are sold on the top shelf and to over-18s only by convention.

At what age can I rent or buy a DVD/video?

DVDs/videos should legally only be supplied, lent or sold to those over the age limit displayed on the DVD/video. There are no legal penalties for showing DVDs/videos in the home to an inappropriate age group.

What sort of pornography is illegal?

Pornographic material is considered legally 'obscene' if it is judged to have 'a tendency to deprave and corrupt' the intended audience. (Obscene Publications Acts 1959 & 1964, as amended). This normally applies only to the most violent and degrading adult pornography. It is currently an offence to 'publish' obscene

material. The Criminal Justice and Immigration Act 2008 has introduced a new offence of being in possession of 'extreme pornographic material'.

Possession of child pornography ('indecent' photographs of children under the age of 18) is a serious criminal offence under the Protection of Children Act 1978 and section 160 of the Criminal Justice Act 1988.

Am I criminally liable if I download pornography?

It depends on what sort of pornography you are downloading. If you knowingly downloaded child pornography, you would be committing a criminal offence.

What happens if I download pornography in my workplace?

It depends on the policy of your employer. Many employers have policies that state downloading pornography or sending inappropriate emails will lead to a disciplinary warning or dismissal.

What should I do if I come across material that I believe to be illegal?

If you come across material that depicts child sexual abuse or material that you think may fall foul of the Obscene Publications Act, you should report it through the Internet Watch Foundation (IWF) hotline. Go to their website, www.iwf.org.uk, where you can make a report online. If you suspect inappropriate chat or behaviour with a child online, you should report to it the Child Exploitation and Online Protection Centre. You can make a report on their website, www.ceop.gov.uk
December 2008

⇨ The above information is reprinted with kind permission from CARE. Visit www.care.org.uk for more information.

Ban on extreme images comes into force

Information from Out-Law.com

It has become illegal in most of the UK to own extreme pornographic images. A new law came into force making it a criminal offence to possess the images in England, Wales and Northern Ireland. A similar law is proposed in Scotland.

The only images that it has been illegal to possess until now have been images of child sexual abuse. It has been an offence to publish obscene images, but not to possess them.

The new law, which is part of the Criminal Justice and Immigration Act of 2008, came into force on 26th January. The Scottish law is being drafted and will go further, criminalising the possession of images of rape.

Though the law has now come into force outside of Scotland it is unlikely to be aggressively enforced. The Association of Chief Police Officers (ACPO) has said that it will not pursue offenders, but will investigate any instances that it comes across of images that break the new law.

ACPO told *The Guardian* newspaper that the police 'will not be actively targeting members of the public but will be conducting investigations into the unlawful possession of this material where found'.

A statement from ACPO's lead officer on extreme pornographic images Jim Gamble said that the new law 'will assist law enforcement officers when presented with future investigations where indecent and illegal material is found'.

'Whilst the publication and distribution of extreme pornography is already covered in UK legislation through the Obscene Publications Act 1959, the new criminal offence of possession of this material has been created in order to prevent the further circulation of what is sexually violent and extreme in nature,' said Gamble. 'It also reflects the potential damaging impact that the possession of this material could have.'

The law says that it is an offence to be in possession of an extreme pornographic image.

'An image is "pornographic" if it is of such a nature that it must reasonably be assumed to have been produced solely or principally for the purpose of sexual arousal,' says the law.

'An "extreme image" is an image which is grossly offensive, disgusting or otherwise of an obscene character'

'An "extreme image" is an image which is grossly offensive, disgusting or otherwise of an obscene character... and if it portrays, in an explicit and realistic way, any of the following –

(a) an act which threatens a person's life,

(b) an act which results, or is likely to result, in serious injury to a person's anus, breasts or genitals,

(c) an act which involves sexual interference with a human corpse, or

(d) a person performing an act of intercourse or oral sex with an animal (whether dead or alive),

and a reasonable person looking at the image would think that any such person or animal was real.'

The Ministry of Justice has said that there are defences to prosecution under the law for those who do not ask for or keep images that are banned under the Act.

Guidance produced by the Ministry said that there is a defence available for 'a person [who] was in possession of an extreme image but had not looked at it and therefore neither knew, nor had reason to suspect that it was an extreme pornographic image; this will cover those who are in possession of offending images but are unaware of the nature of the images: for example, where a person is sent an electronic copy of an image which he saves without looking at it and which gave rise to no suspicion that it might be extreme pornography'.

It said that there was also a defence for people who had been sent the message but did not ask for it, and who deleted it quickly. This is a defence even if the person looked at the image, it said.

Anyone found guilty under the Act could be jailed for three years and be ordered to pay an unlimited fine. They may also be placed on the sex offenders' register.
29 January 2009

⇨ The above information first appeared on OUT-LAW.COM, part of international law firm Pinsent Masons LLP, on 29 January 2009. It has been reproduced with permission. Visit www.out-law.com for more information.

Warning! Adult content, you must be at least 18 years old to enter this site

Criminalising extreme porn

Feminists are split over government plans to ban so-called extreme porn, with some groups arguing censorship is not a real solution to the wider social problem of violence against women. By Katy Taylor

A bid to prevent people viewing images of rape and sexual violence has split opinion among feminists, with strong opposition being voiced within some sections of the women's movement.

Justice Secretary Jack Straw wants to make owning, downloading or viewing bestiality, necrophilia or severe sexual violence illegal as of next January via an amendment to the Criminal Justice and Immigration Act.

A bid to prevent people viewing images of rape and sexual violence has split opinion

The move has won the support of many women who believe it will help reduce gender violence. Dr Sasha Rakoff, director of lobby group Object, said: 'We are not talking about fluffy Ann Summers' handcuffs here, we are talking about the depiction of rape, mutilation and abuse so graphic that it is impossible to tell whether or not it is real or simulated.

'The case against banning the possession of such material is deeply flawed and misleading.'

Many have argued against the proposals though; on 22 October a handful of protesters demonstrated outside parliament, calling for the government to 'ban crime, not sex'.

This opposition is deeply disturbing, Rakoff argues, in a society where one in three women experience male violence, and where sexual violence has become increasingly mainstreamed in the porn industry and wider society.

That abuse of women is unacceptable is not up for debate.

As Rakoff said: 'The feminist point of view is a human rights point of view.' How best to tackle it involves ongoing argument, however.

Laura Schwarz of Feminist Fightback said: 'To focus on porn as the primary cause of violence against women is not only reductive and simplistic but politically dangerous. It prevents a more in-depth analysis of the causes of sexual violence and ignores other forms of violence – police violence, state violence or the violence of the capitalist system.'

Avedon Carol, of Feminists Against Censorship (FAC), goes further: 'This legislation only has value in a police state because it does not do anything to prevent violence against women. It suppresses sexuality, which can only create more problems later.'

The planned law changes have come about following the murder of Jane Longhurst in 2003 by Graham Coutts – a man who was addicted to violent porn sites.

Longhurst's mother, Liz, has argued easy access to extreme online images had tipped her daughter's killer over the edge.

However, there is little evidence to show there has been an increase in violence against women with the increase in availability of images depicting it, on the Internet and elsewhere. This argument is repeated by those who feel the amendments are a token effort that avoid the root problem of violence against women.

Female porn director, Yoshki Greenberg, is a rarity. She is one of a small handful of women who stand behind the camera on the film set, rather than lie in front of it. Perhaps more surprisingly she makes (consensual) 'niche narrative' films, some of which may be affected by the new legislation that will ban pictures of slavery or captivity.

Despite the violent nature of some of her films she was vehemently against abuse of women, although she shared Object's opinion that 'porn as punishment' films are increasingly popular with the mainstream.

She said increased censorship won't help: 'I obviously have no issue with the quest to reduce violence, I just don't think this will achieve it. To ban extreme porn is to ignore the issues of why people want to watch it in the first place – what it is that triggers violent behaviour in people.'

Erotic photographer and ex-escort Karen, who won Sex Worker of the Year in 2004 for setting up an ethical escort agency, believes the move will have absolutely no effect on increasing women's safety, in the sex industry or otherwise, but is rather about increasing government control over our lives.

Straw rejects this. He has said the government's intention is to combat the circulation of extreme pornographic images, not to limit private sexual activity. Ministers point to the consultation paper which indicated men who were predisposed to aggression or sexual violence were more susceptible to the influence of extreme porn.

But FAC's Avedon Carol claimed: 'It happens every time there is a real concern about violence against women, the government think they can soothe it by eliminating pictures of violence against women. It's not tackling the real issue.'

Of course the vast majority of women who experience violence and sexual abuse do so from someone they know.

Perhaps prioritising Rape Crisis Centres, tackling domestic violence and ensuring effective prosecution would help far more than criminalising the small minority who enjoy extreme porn.

But then it would also cost a lot more money.

28 October 2008

⇨ Information from the *New Statesman*. Visit www.newstatesman.com for more information.

© *New Statesman*

Jane Austen and the case for extreme porn

The debate on a proposed offence of possessing extreme images has drawn an argument from an unlikely source

Jane Austen seems an unlikely standard-bearer for those who defend the right to look at images depicting women being tortured and raped.

The novelist was quoted during a conference at Durham University this week, which debated proposed legislation that would make possession of 'extreme pornography' a criminal offence carrying a three-year prison sentence.

The decision to introduce a new law followed a long campaign by a mother whose daughter was killed in 2003 by a man who was said to have been an obsessive viewer of violent porn sites.

Supporters of the new sanction, part of the Criminal Justice Bill that is due to be brought before the Commons in the next few months, see it as a logical extension of laws against child pornography.

The proposed offence covers explicit images of bestiality, necrophilia and serious violence, defined as 'acts that appear to be life-threatening or are likely to result in serious, disabling injury'. Such material must have been created solely or primarily for the purpose of sexual arousal, and must show real scenes 'or depictions which appear to be real acts'.

It is already illegal to publish or distribute such images in Britain. The Home Office argues that making their possession illegal will give added protection to the young and vulnerable. Opposition among politicians to the new law is likely to be muted. Brave or foolish would be the MP prepared to defend publicly the material shown on a website such as Necrobabes. The site promises users 'tastefully erotic death scenes through asphyxia, shooting, knives and more'.

A sister website, Asphyxia, lures

By Andrew Norfolk

browsers with the slogan: 'Sexy strangled, suffocated, hanged and drowned babes. It takes your breath away.' What sane person could defend the rights of someone who gains arousal from the sight of women being humiliated, degraded and — apparently — murdered?

Backlash claims that 'hundreds of thousands, if not millions, of people engaged in non-abusive, consenting activities' would be criminalised by a ban on extreme porn

---

Step forward Austen, or rather the eponymous heroine of *Emma* as she remarks to her father: 'One half of the world cannot understand the pleasures of the other.' Those words went to the heart of the debate during the conference at Durham, 'Positions on the Politics of Porn', which drew together a range of groups — from law professors to bondage aficionados —

with a special interest in the proposed new offence.

The argument went something like this: I may not understand your sexuality, indeed I may find the images you like to view grotesque and repugnant, but is that sufficient reason to criminalise the act of viewing? All parties agreed that possessing Internet footage of, for example, a genuine strangulation should be unlawful.

Far more contentious were scenes involving actors or consensual partners, where the explicit footage appears to show a violent asphyxiation but is actually the realistic playing out of a fantasy. Under the proposals, it would be illegal to possess such images.

Rightly so, according to Jill Radford of the University of Teesside, who views all pornography as 'the eroticisation of hate' and a symbol of 'male domination and exploitation of women and children'.

Porn was 'a significant and pervasive factor in shaping our understanding of sexuality', she said, and when it came to images of extreme violence the issue of consent was irrelevant because the message — that it was legitimate to use violence against women — remained the same. Gavin Phillipson, of Durham University, also backed the legislation. The actors may be consenting participants, but

if the scenes simulate non-consensual acts, and are produced solely for the purpose of arousing the viewer, the images are not a legitimate use of freedom of expression.

Professor Phillipson said that the 'very narrow and specific categories' of the law would protect members of the BDSM (bondage, domination and sado-masochism) community who held true to the 'sacred principles' of safety and consent.

Deborah Hyde was not convinced. A spokesperson for Backlash, a group formed to fight the legislation, she described the proposal as 'a law based on prejudice rather than fact'. Backlash claims that 'hundreds of thousands, if not millions, of people engaged in non-abusive, consenting

activities' would be criminalised by a ban on extreme porn.

The suggestion that there may be a causal link between pornography and sexual violence is not supported by any authoritative research, as the Government has admitted.

For Avedon Carol, of Feminists Against Censorship, this means that 'we're going to ruin people's lives without a shred of evidence that it [viewing extreme porn] harms anyone. We are trying to punish people who might have fantasies that we don't like. It's a thought crime and that's all it is.'

So as long as no one is physically harmed, pornography is acceptable? Not so, according to Clare Phillipson, of Wearside Women in Need. 'I'm not

going to sit here and be an apologist for a psychopath's right to w***,' she said. 'This is about real women. You people need to get real.'

She went on to claim that hundreds of African women had been trafficked into Europe, then sold, mutilated and murdered, their deaths being filmed and photographed to cater for the market in extreme pornography.

'Anyone turned on by the glorification of extreme violence is sick. It sends a message to abhorrent individuals that it is acceptable. What [the Government] are doing is censoring evil. I will not get lost in a debate about human rights on this. There are some things that are just wrong.'
17 March 2007

Change society and porn will change too

Fiona Osler says she's no prude but don't discount the effect porn has on individuals and society

It's not fashionable these days to take an anti-porn stance. The accusation that you're aligning yourself with the fundamentalist Christian right is never far away. However, it is possible to argue that there is quite a lot wrong with porn and not be a moralist, a man-hater or a prude. You don't have to believe

all men are rapists to acknowledge that much pornography reinforces the male domination already found elsewhere in society.

I'm not advocating a ban on porn but to say porn needs to be honestly re-evaluated without the moralising or hysteria that so often accompanies this discussion. I have no issues with

non-degrading images or porn that isn't just about what humiliating things a man can do to a woman. But how much of this type of porn exists compared to porn that shows only contempt, sexualises inequality and eroticises male supremacy?

It's not fashionable these days to take an anti-porn stance

"Problem? No, I don't have a problem with porn."

Supporting the porn industry

Porn is most often unrelentingly misogynistic; it doesn't celebrate women's sexuality or speak of empowerment, as some on the left would argue. The fact is, porn is invariably made by men for men and for the main part says women exist to cater to male sexual needs and desires. Even if porn holds no consequences for relationships between men and women, why is the left supporting a business that controls our sexuality? That also promotes racism as much as sexism? Yet seeing this in a pornographic film is met with silence or the standard anti-censorship arguments that people have a right to look at what they want.

It is possible to argue that there is quite a lot wrong with porn and not be a moralist, a man-hater or a prude

The relaxation of the British Board of Film Classification guidelines in 2000 means hardcore pornography is available as never before. A 2006 study, commissioned by the *Independent on Sunday*, found one in four men aged 25 to 49 (around 2.5 million) had viewed online hardcore porn in the month the study was conducted. And as the porn industry exhausts every conceivable sexual scenario, there is only one place left to go – porn focusing on cruelty and extreme degradation of women. It's no longer about sex but hate.

It's dishonest and misleading to claim pornography has no effect on relationships. Relate report that 40 per cent of couples who come to them cite Internet pornography as a contributory factor to their problems – are they making it up or can we accept it has an effect? I'm not saying all men and women are personally affected by porn but it is also disingenuous to claim that if a society accepts any genre that portrays women in solely sexual terms it will not influence to a greater or lesser degree how some men treat us and how some women respond to them.

These days, young men are learning from pornography that women enjoy forced sex, humiliation and cruelty. This is not the soft porn of *Playboy* or *Penthouse* and often it's before they have any involvement with young women. At a time when developing empathy and intimacy skills are crucial to mature sexual and emotional interactions they are viewing porn which is all about self-gratification, often at the expense of a woman's pain and suffering. That women are always 'up for it' in turn puts enormous pressure on young women to conform to the plasticised images and obligated to 'perform' no matter how objectionable they find the act.

Response to the new sexual parity?

Some psychologists have posited that men who seek more extreme images feel threatened by the 'emotional power' they believe women hold over them. This means they are reliant on women finding them sexually attractive and emotionally acceptable.

How much easier if women are always 'hot to trot,' in a world where male authority goes unchallenged, where there is no need for intimacy and trust. Intimacy demands sharing and is built on varying levels of trust. Love, sensuality, tenderness, caring and empathy are emotions entirely absent from the porn genre. Cruelty, anger and hatred aplenty.

Why do men want to look at this? I confess I don't understand it. I'm not arguing all men looking at this kind of porn hate women but there is obviously a market for it or it wouldn't be produced. Is it a reaction to new sexual parity? It hurts me to think that some men see women as the enemy, that they hold such contempt and hatred, and gain sexual gratification from seeing women used in this way.

There are no easy answers as to what can be done. I have always been anti-censorship but perhaps we need legislation that outlaws any pornography that incites sexual hatred similar to laws that outlaw race hatred? But more than this, we need to try harder to ensure men and women treat each other with respect and equality, this has to come first before porn will change.
January 2008

⇨ The above information is reprinted with kind permission from Red Pepper. Visit www.redpepper.org.uk for more information.
© *Red Pepper*

Worldwide pornography revenues

2006 worldwide pornography revenues (as percentage of total):

UK – 2%
Italy – 1%
Australia – 2%
Canada, Philippines, Taiwan, Germany, Finland, Czech Republic, Russia, Netherlands, Brazil – 5%
US 14%
China 28%
Japan 21%
South Korea 27%

Pornography time statistics

- Every second $3,075.64 is being spent on pornography.
- Every second 28,258 Internet users are viewing pornography.
- Every second 372 Internet users are typing adult search terms into search engines.
- Every 39 minutes a new pornographic video is being created in the United States.

Source: TopTenREVIEWS, March 2007. Photograph from Stock Xchng (by analyser).

Sex object culture

Frequently asked questions from Object

'Research suggests that the sexualisation of girls may not only reflect sexist attitudes, a societal tolerance of sexual violence, and the exploitation of girls and women but may also contribute to these phenomena'.
Report of the American Psychological Association Task Force on the Sexualisation of Girls, 2007

What do we mean by sex object culture?

You only have to go to your local corner shop or supermarket, turn on MTV, jump on a bus to get to school or work, and you will be bombarded with images of women in highly sexualised poses and with vacant expressions being used to sell products, music and films.

Girls are targeted at younger and younger ages as consumers of sex object culture. WH Smith sell pink Playboy pencil cases – yet Playboy is a global pornography brand; Amazon sell pole dancing kits with paper money as toys; Tesco even sell 'Porn Star' T-shirts for 3- to 6-month-old girls. Celebrities endorse the pornography industry and glamour models are held out as role models for young girls. The message is loud and clear: to be validated as a female, you have to be 'hot'. This is increasingly the case as pornography and the sex industries (such as prostitution or lap dancing) become part of our mainstream culture and everyday lives.

Doesn't Object just have a problem with sex?

It's not sex we have a problem with – it is the sexualisation of women and girls in a way which has little parallel for men or boys. And it's not sex that's everywhere – it is images that originate from pornography. Sex and pornography are very different, although the mission of lads' mags and the like is to persuade

us otherwise. When campaigners criticise McDonalds for its unhealthy food, environmentally destructive business practices and targeting of children through manipulative marketing, does anybody accuse them of being anti-food?

But, isn't it all just a bit of harmless fun?

The sexualisation of women in the media and mainstreaming of the sex industry is filling the gap of sex education and shaping how sexual identities are formed. Alarmingly, 66% of young people say that they find out about sex, love and relationships through the media (Institute of Education, 2003). This is harmful. As pornography saturates mainstream culture and the line between what used to be considered hardcore and what is sold in newsagents and supermarket becomes increasingly blurred, the rape narrative which originated from porn has become increasingly acceptable.

In fact, *Maxim* (2006) even tells teenage readers that 'a lot of women fantasise about things like being raped' and that 'it's a myth that women like soft stuff'. This message is reflected by statistics showing that almost half of all adult women in England and Wales have experienced domestic violence, sexual assault or stalking (British Crime Survey 2004) and a high proportion of people still think that women are at least partially to blame for rape, with rape conviction rates at an all-time low (Amnesty International, 2005).

'Sex object culture' also harms boys who are pressurised to act out a version of 'being a man' in which power over women is normal. The effect is demonstrated by the fact that only 8% of rapes are stranger rapes. The vast majority of rape is carried out by women's current or former partners. This means that it is 'ordinary' boys and men who are committing sexually violent crimes. The media's portrayal of women as sex objects also harms girls' mental and physical health, leading to a lack of confidence with their bodies as well as eating disorders (American Psychological Association, 2007). Women and girls are comparing themselves with celebrities who have had plastic surgery and whose photographs have been airbrushed. It is no wonder that in the UK at least one million people have eating disorders (approximately 90% of whom are women) and that upwards of one billion pounds is spent on plastic surgery annually (approximately 90% of which is spent by women).

The message is loud and clear: to be validated as a female, you have to be 'hot'

When women are overwhelmingly valued on the basis of their looks this has an impact on all spheres of life. Is it any wonder that Parliament is 80% male, and that the gender pay gap means that in effect women are only paid until October of each year compared to men? The one-dimensional representation of women also reinforces racism – by promoting stereotyped ideals of white, hypersexualised women. This ideal fails to represent the true diversity of women in the UK.

But what if it's a woman's choice to be a glamour model or lap dancer?

Mainstream media outlets glamorise the 'porn star' life. For example, even though extensive research shows that prostitution is all too frequently abusive and exploitative, the media story is still one of the 'Belle du Jour' fantasy of a successful and glamorous 'call girl'. Instead of showing the realities of lap dancing, page 3 or prostitution, the media focuses on discussions on women's choice to participate in the sex industry.

Actually, the issue of choice is complex. We have to look at all the factors which influence our choices, including the way that the media and popular culture glamorises the sex industry. Even if we could establish that it truly was a genuine and empowering choice of a woman to go into one of these industries, the harmful impact that their normalisation has on society makes the issue much bigger than one of individual choice.

What about freedom of speech?

We are talking about multi-billion pound media and sex industries backed up by big business. It is clear that it is the sex industry and all those making profit out of sex object culture that have the loudest voice. It is the women and men who want to challenge this culture that are silenced. We are not calling for censorship. Object is calling for improved regulation of the media in

Is it a woman's right to become a glamour model if she chooses?

relation to sexism and for people to understand the reality and effects of normalising words and images which reinforce and normalise inequalities between women and men. Quite rightly this has been recognised in the arena of racial equality, where legislation criminalises the incitement of racial hatred.

Isn't it time for such laws to be brought in to protect the rights of women?

⇨ The above information is reprinted with kind permission from Object. Visit www.object.org.uk for more information.

© Object

MPs want age ratings for lads' mags

Politicians want to give so-called 'lads' mags' and newspapers such as the *Daily Sport* cinema-style age ratings

The *Top Shelf* report, out this week, recommends magazines such as *Zoo* and *Maxim* carry '16' or '18' certificates.

The report, which has cross-party support from MPs, found newsagents were flouting guidelines which say the magazines should be displayed on the top shelf.

The display of the magazines is governed by a voluntary code of practice drawn up by the Periodical Publishers Associations (PPA) and the Home Office, which recommends that retailers display them well above children's eye level and away from children's titles or comics.

'The industry has manifestly failed to control the display of sexually-explicit material,' said Labour MP Claire Curtis-Thomas.

'We need to have age-related information put on the front of all lads' magazines.'

The MP for Crosby, who has spent a year and a half researching the industry, said: 'It is clear that young men below the age of 16 have access to these magazines.

'I do not want to censor this material, but we must do something about the display of these titles.

'The discretionary industry guidelines have failed. Children are still able to access material that is of a sexually explicit and violent nature.

'We want to introduce statutory guidelines that are comparable to the existing standards for video, film and television.'

But the PPA says a voluntary code is 'far more effective and flexible than any statutory regulation'.

The report surveyed sixth form students and found that all the girls who looked at the *Daily Sport*, *Zoo* and *Nuts* reported being angry, offended or upset by the images they contained.

Only 11% of male students said they felt the same, but one-fifth admitted the material encouraged them to see women as sex objects.

Ben Todd, editor of *Zoo*, said: 'We should be treated like a cheeky seaside postcard.

'In our case, the most revealing aspect is topless pictures, which is no more than you see in the *Sun* or the *Daily Star*.

'So, if any sort of age restrictions are going to be introduced, I'd expect them to include those papers too.'

8 December 2008

⇨ The above information is reprinted with kind permission from Sky News. Visit http://news.sky.com for more information.

© Sky News

Lads' mags

Frequently asked questions from Object

What exactly are you campaigning for?

We are campaigning for lads' mags and newspapers like the *Sport* to be recognised and regulated as part of the porn industry and not displayed at eye level next to magazines, comics and broadsheet newspapers as if they were a normal part of the mainstream media.

> It is clear that these publications are part of the sex and porn industries and they should be recognised and regulated as such

We think that if lads' mags and newspapers like the *Sport* are sold at all, they should be covered up, put on the top shelf and that age restrictions should be applied. This would send out the message that as a society we do not think that it is acceptable for women to be objectified, demeaned and degraded and that we do not condone it as part of our mainstream media.

Why do you say that lads' mags are part of the porn industry?

Links to hardcore pornography and prostitution are made explicit in the pages of ads at the back of every lads' mag and essentially the entire content of the *Sport* (which comprises thousands of ads for hardcore porn, sex chat, masseurs and escorts). But even without these direct links, the purpose of lads' mags and papers like the *Sport* is to sexually stimulate male readers by turning women into sexual objects who are always sexually available and who represent the 'porn dream'. Lads' mags also publish articles specifically about pornography. For example, in 2006

Zoo published an A-Z of pornography which included wrapping your girlfriend in cling film and defecating on her. It also included lots of references to women as the 'B' word with advice on how to deal with your 'B' if she doesn't comply. It is clear that these publications are part of the sex and porn industries and they should be recognised and regulated as such to take into account the harmful effect that they have on how women are viewed.

Aren't lads' mags just a bit of harmless fun?

Lads' mags provide sexual stimulation by portraying women as sexual objects who are always sexually available and whose purpose is to fulfil the sexual fantasies of men. They are directly linked to hardcore pornography and prostitution through their advertising and they constantly trivialise or make fun of issues like rape, trafficking and prostituting women.

This is especially alarming when we consider that 66% of children and young people say that they find out about sex, love and relationships through the media (Institute of Education 2003). Do we want young people who are shaping their sexual identities to be learning about sexuality from magazines like *Maxim* (2006), who advised male readers

that 'most women fantasise about being raped' and that 'it's a myth that women like soft sex'?

But this isn't only a question of protecting children from these harmful messages. Lads' mags promote a warped view of how women are supposed to look and behave sexually which is damaging for us all, as they influence the way that men view women and the way that women view themselves. Take 2005 – the height of the lads' mag boom – when *Zoo* ran a competition where male readers could win breast implants for their girlfriends and *Nuts* started the infamous 'Assess my Breasts' competition with readers' girlfriends being encouraged to send in photographs of their breasts to be graded by male readers. In this year the number of women who had breast implants doubled (British Association of Aesthetic Plastic Surgeons, 2006).

When we live in a society in which 92% of girls under 22 say that 'they hate their bodies' (*Bliss*, 2005), 63% of girls say that they would rather be glamour models than teachers or doctors (Manchester Online, 2005), the UK spends more on cosmetic surgery than any other EU country – of which approximately 90% is spent by women (Mintel, 2008), one in four women are raped in their lifetime with 92% of rapes committed by 'ordinary' boys and men who are known to the woman (Kelly, Lovett and Regan, 2005), and the positions of power in society are still overwhelmingly dominated by men, can we really say with confidence that portraying women as sexual objects is just harmless fun and has no effect whatsoever on the attitudes behind these statistics?

63% of girls say that they would rather be glamour models than teachers or doctors

---

But women choose to do it?

Indeed, 63% of girls say that they would rather be glamour models than teachers or doctors. We find these findings alarming as it says a great deal about the kinds of aspirations that are being held out for women in our society.

But glamour models make a lot of money?

Out of the thousands of women who aspire to be glamour models, very, very few actually 'make it'.

Even if it were the case that every woman who aspired to be a glamour model 'got rich', what would that say about our society if the majority of women (the 63% who aspire to this profession) stripped off to look sexy as their profession whilst all the positions of power were still overwhelmingly dominated by men?

Is that the kind of society that we want?

Surely we need to question why girls are aspiring to be glamour models rather than politicians, teachers, doctors or any other position of real influence. Here we have to look at the way that publications such as lads' mags glamorise the porn industry.

What about freedom of speech/censorship?

This is an equality issue not an issue of freedom of speech. In the same way that boycotting/not giving a platform to racist views is making a political decision to challenge deeply entrenched racism, boycotting and not giving a platform to sexist views is a way of challenging deeply entrenched sexism. Opposing the sexist portrayal of women in the media is taking a political stance against sexism, it is not censorship.

Does opposing lad's mags mean you are anti-sex?

Challenging the pornification of society and sex object culture does not make you anti-sex, it just means that you are pointing out the danger of continuing to represent women as sex objects who are always sexually available in a culture in which sexual violence is so endemic. It makes you are anti-sexism, not anti-sex.

Wouldn't these regulations take us back to the Dark Ages?

These measures are about recognising and regulating publications like lad's mags and the *Sport* for what they are

and recognising the harmful effects of mainstreaming pornography and the sexual objectification of women.

The issue of challenging the objectification of women is an issue of equality which is a progressive ideal. It is the sexist attitudes that lads mags promote that belong in the past.

Why is the objectification of women an issue?

Objectification dehumanises women. The first part of any oppression is to dehumanise the group which is oppressed. The more it becomes acceptable to view women as a sum of body parts, over which men have entitlement the easier it becomes to disrespect, to mistreat and to act out violence and sexual harassment towards women as a group.

We are not saying that all men who read degrading materials about women will have sexist views, let alone be abusive or violent, but when we live in a society in which gender inequality is massive and violence against women is endemic – with one in four women raped in her lifetime and two women dying each week from domestic violence (Rape Crisis) – any industry which promotes the objectification of women inevitably has an impact on the sexist attitudes which underpin abuse and cannot be said to be harmless.

⇨ The above information is reprinted with kind permission from Object. Visit www.object.org.uk for more information.

© Object

Why lads' mags have a shelf life

Michael Deacon argues that lads' mags are harmless fun, not misogyny, drawing on two years of experience at *Zoo* magazine

From its launch in January 2004 until November 2006, I worked for *Zoo*, the weekly lads' magazine. Please don't be alarmed. I have no plans to bring its twin selling-points of topless glamour models and gurgling puerility to the pages of the *Daily Telegraph*. I bring up this charming period from my past only because Claire Curtis-Thomas, Labour MP for Crosby, has announced that she wants to prevent teenage boys from buying *Zoo* and its cheerfully crude kind.

Hardcore pornography is dingy, aggressive, and, above all, serious. Lads' magazines are not

Curtis-Thomas has compiled a report demanding that 'lads' mags' carry cinema-style age ratings. By 'lads' mags' she means not the sort of pornographic publication available only from a newsagent's top shelf and usually sheathed in a polythene bag. She's talking about what are, in theory at any rate, mainstream 'lifestyle' magazines by mainstream publishers: *Zoo*, *Nuts*, *FHM* and others that grew out of the men's magazine phenomenon of the mid-to-late Nineties.

All of them are freely available in newsagents, at a height a pubescent boy could reach. And all contain a lot of photographs of topless women. Nonetheless, I don't think that these magazines deserve our ire. Rude they may be. Pitiable, in many respects. But dangerous, threatening, malign? No.

Allow me to explain.

At *Zoo*, I was the deputy enter-tainment editor. Not the most appropriate title, perhaps, because my job was to write and edit reviews of television programmes and films and CDs, and I am well aware that these do not constitute the primary source of entertainment for which young men buy the magazine.

But, even though its pages were bursting with topless photographs, I wasn't embarrassed by *Zoo*. Well, all right, I sometimes was. But not because I thought the magazine was obscene, but because, at times, our efforts to produce it were so comical. The flaw of the lads' magazine, as a genre, is that it is almost always produced by men who are nothing like its target readers. In fact, it's produced by men who were probably beaten up at school by its target readers' fathers. Producing a lads' magazine is a perpetual fluster of second-guessing. In a senior editorial meeting, university-educated, middle-class men in their thirties try to squeeze themselves into the mindset of a 19-year-old squaddie from Nuneaton. Picture the publishing world the other way round. Picture Wayne Rooney editing *Tatler*.

Today *Zoo* is edited by Ben Todd (who arrived after I left). Todd defends his magazine and its rivals by saying they're no more obscene than 'a cheeky seaside postcard'. At first this may sound disingenuous. But actually I think he has a point. Because, like a 'cheeky seaside postcard', lads' magazines are not erotic. They're stuffed with sex yet not at all sexy. They are, instead, a chortling compendium of banalities. They are unrelentingly silly. Indeed, their silliness is almost a kind of innocence.

Look at last week's issue of *Nuts*. (It's all right, you don't actually have to look – I've done it for you.) The cover promises a naked shoot with a model from Cheshire. 'Ey-up,' squeaks the headline, 'they're my naughtiest ever pics!'

Inside, photographs of topless women are routinely adorned with off-puttingly twee quotations from accompanying interviews. These include 'I like to wear cute French knickers!' and, almost touchingly, 'A girl not wanting to talk to you isn't the end of the world!'.

Hardcore pornography is dingy, aggressive, and, above all, serious.

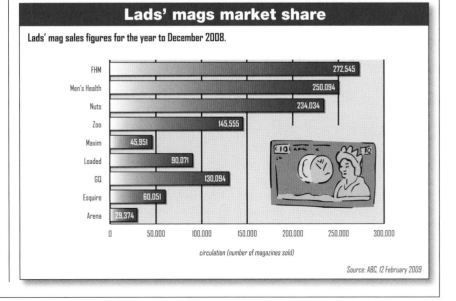

Lads' mags market share

Lads' mag sales figures for the year to December 2008.

Magazine	Circulation
FHM	272,545
Men's Health	250,094
Nuts	234,034
Zoo	145,555
Maxim	45,951
Loaded	90,071
GQ	130,094
Esquire	60,051
Arena	29,374

circulation (number of magazines sold)

Source: ABC, 12 February 2009

Lads' magazines are not. They're naff. They're juvenile. They're downright giggly with nerves. Look, boys: it's an actual lady! She's taken her clothes off! And she doesn't mind if we look!

That attitude may be pitiful but I don't think it's cruel or misogynistic, and I don't think we need age classifications to prevent teenage boys from being exposed to it.

Misogyny is hatred of women. *Nuts*, *Zoo*, *FHM* and the rest do not encourage their readers to hate women. They encourage them to be hopelessly in thrall to the sight of women's breasts. No, that's not a healthy attitude either, but it could be a lot worse.

Difficult though it may be to believe today, lads' magazines were not always crammed with nudity. The first of their kind, *Loaded*, began publishing in 1994. Its early cover stars were often men, the sort of men its editors imagined its readers looked up to: raffish, roguish types, such as Paul Gascoigne, the Oasis guitarist Noel Gallagher and the Madness singer Suggs.

The tone of the magazine during these early years was arch, witty, tongue-in-cheek - relatively sophisticated. It wasn't intimidating. It didn't set out to shock. It just didn't want to apologise for enjoying laddish pursuits - which included publishing pictures of attractive actresses in their underwear.

In time, however, *Loaded*'s rival *FHM* made an intriguing discovery: if you put a picture of a naked young woman on the cover, your magazine sold more copies. A lot more copies. One month in 1999, *FHM*'s cover star was the children's television presenter Gail Porter. She was shot naked, from the rear. The issue sold more than a million copies. No editor was going to go back to Suggs after that.

Nor would they today. Because the sales of lads' magazines are in decline - rapid decline. The latest figures, published in August, showed that every lads' magazine had lost at least 10 per cent of its readers in the past year. *Maxim*, remarkably, had lost 59.6 per cent. Nowadays, the pictures of topless girls aren't there to increase a magazine's circulation - they're there to ensure that the magazine has a circulation at all.

Critics may like to think that the reason that readers are deserting these publications is that they're fed up with the puerility, and would return if a more tasteful alternative appeared. But it just isn't true. Throughout the time I worked for *Zoo*, its sales lagged behind those of *Nuts*. At the end of 2005, a new editor arrived. He was going to increase sales by decreasing the nudity. Out went the nipples - and down went the sales. Not much later, the nipples came back.

Even so, sales across the board are still sliding. This isn't because young men have lost interest in pictures of naked women. On the contrary - it's because they now have easy access to even more of them. The Internet offers far more sexually explicit images, and offers them faster. Monthly and weekly magazines can't compete.

You may think that to impose age limits on lads' magazines is a laudable idea. Perhaps it is, but it's also futile. You can stop a teenage boy buying a magazine in a newsagent but there's not much you can do to stop him looking at far more graphic images on the Internet.

If sales of lads' magazines continue their decline, then in a few years they may not be available to anyone, let alone teenage boys. But teenage boys will still be looking at pornography. The argument against lads' magazines may be just, or it may be overblown and prudish - but either way, it's too late.

18 December 2008

Should lap dancing be run out of town?

With a new venue opening every week, lap dancing has spread into British culture. Rachel Cooke talks to the men behind the boom, the women lured by the promise of easy money, and the campaigners battling to stop the clubs opening on your doorstep

The lap-dancing industry will tell you that its 10,000 (their estimate) female employees are all as happy as Larry: that its 'performers' are decently paid and well looked after, and enjoy some of the most flexible working in Britain.

But I am not so sure. The first time I call Lucy, an ex-lap dancer, she says: 'I think you must have the wrong number' and hangs up, fast. The second time - by now she has remembered who I am and why I want to talk to her - she tells me: 'I'd rather not say what I am doing these days, for the same reason that I won't tell you my real name. These are people [the club owners] you don't want to mess with. I am genuinely afraid of them. Who knows exactly what goes on behind the scenes, but I'd still rather not mess with it.'

Lucy began lap dancing when she lost her job as an office temp. It was quite simple: she needed to pay her rent. 'It felt like a desperate decision,' she says. 'It was a case of: I can't do anything else. But also I'd fallen for the myth that lap dancing is a good way of making a lot of money very quickly.' She applied for, and got, a job as a dancer in a supposedly upmarket club. At the end of her first night's work, however, she went home having earned nothing at all. More alarmingly, she now owed the club some £80. Like the vast majority of lap dancers in the UK, Lucy was self-employed. Not only was she required to pay the club a dance fee every time she wanted to work, a sum that could vary from £10 to £80 (Friday nights were most expensive, because they were most popular with customers), but she also had to give the club commission on every dance performed (nude dances cost punters £20, of which she kept £17.50; on slow nights, she might perform only once or twice, or not at all). And then there were the fines. 'You got fined for everything, at £20 a time: if you were late, if you were wearing the wrong shoes or dress, if you failed to dance on the pole twice an hour. There was also a fine if you were caught breaking the 3ft rule [licensing laws require dancers to stay 3ft away from customers] – though strangely, that one they never seemed to enforce.'

In 2008 a lap-dancing club opened in Britain almost every week

Lucy lasted for six months. 'It was very hard to make money: it was like having a very competitive sales job. They'd filled the shop with loads of the same thing – us, the dancers – and then there'd be only five customers. It wasn't just that we cost them nothing; the more of us there were, the more they made, even if the place was empty. At the end of the night – 2am or whatever – you'd need to take a taxi home, of course. But you'd have to pay for that, too, so I often ended up walking. No one is looking out for you, whatever the clubs say. You're on your own.'

Did any of the women enjoy the work?

'A small number were there because they wanted to move into glamour modelling, and they thought this might be a way in. But for most it was about trying to make enough money to pay their bills. There were problems with drink and drugs; people were using coke and drink, especially drink, quite blatantly, to get hammered.' Partly, she says, this was the only way some women could pluck up enough courage to

undress. 'But it was also extremely boring, and drink made it less so.'

Lap dancers need to tout for business, which means, in effect, chatting men up, flirting. 'You had to have the same tedious conversations over and over and over.' Did she drink? 'Yes. For me, it was for Dutch courage.'

The only way to survive as a dancer, she believes, is to pull a psychological trick on yourself. All lap dancers use a 'dance name' in the clubs. It lends them anonymity, of sorts. But it also gives them a persona to hide behind. 'Brook', 'Jordan' or 'Sasha' is a much more fun, outgoing girl than the woman who plays her, and she favours more outrageous clothes and make-up. Thus, for a time, it is possible to convince yourself that everything is OK. 'No one in the club would express any uncertainty about what they are doing – they're too busy competing for work – so even if you do feel bad about it, you wonder if you are the only one. You convince yourself that your perception of what the job would be like is the same as what the job is, even though there is a quite weird gap between the two. It's only when you have made the decision to leave that you realise how insane it all was.'

And even once you are on the outside, it is not always easy to leave the clubs behind. 'You have to start lying straightaway – as soon as you apply for your next job. There's going to be a gap on your CV. You probably also lie to your family, and your boyfriend, and it affects your relationships. If I had a pretty low opinion of men before I became a lap dancer, it only got worse afterwards. Because you see the worst of men in there.'

What about the club owners' insistence that lap dancing has nothing whatsoever to do with the sex industry? That it is merely part of the entertainment industry? For Lucy, this is laughable. 'Anyone who works in lap dancing and who deludes themselves that they are not a sex worker is in for a shock. No one respects lap dancing. The rest of the world thinks you're a slag.' This would, she thinks, be the case even if all the rules were observed. But, unfortunately, they rarely are. 'Customers might not come in for sex, but it is about sexual stimulation, whatever the clubs say – and it is

physical. It shouldn't even be called dancing. It's not a show. The 3ft rule is a joke. You pay someone to get naked and then grind away on your crotch.'

The pressure to shift boundaries like this is a direct result of the clubs' business model: as freelances, the women who 'do' more earn more. 'In theory, you could decide only to dance on the pole all night, or to dance topless rather than nude (a topless dance is £10, half the price of a 'fully nude' dance). But if you're surrounded by 29 women who will take their pants off, how on earth are you going to make money?'

Since 2003, when the Licensing Act came in, the number of lap-dancing clubs in Britain has almost doubled. There are now some 310 such establishments in the UK, though this figure may not take into account struggling pubs which, their profits battered on one side by the smoking ban and cheap supermarket booze, and on the other by the financial downturn, are now turning to strip nights to keep their businesses alive. In 2008 a lap-dancing club opened in Britain almost every week – last May, five opened for business – and not only in big cities and dreary out-of-town business parks. There are now venues in places such as Worthing and Sidcup, Henley and Stratford-Upon-Avon: small, genteel towns to which people move for the good schools. Residents usually oppose the licensing of such venues, but only rarely do their efforts to persuade the local council to turn down such applications come off. In 2008 only two campaigns were successful: in Durham and West Kensington. In Durham a lap-dancing club, to be operated by Vimac Leisure bang in the middle of the cathedral city, was initially granted a licence by the local council, a shock decision that was only overturned at an appeal for which residents bravely hired their own barrister.

The simple fact is that, tomorrow, you or I or anyone could wake up to find that the licensed premises at the end of our street had turned into, or was shortly about to turn into, a strip venue. Its windows would be blacked out, and that would be it. Or we could discover that one of the big owners – For Your Eyes Only, perhaps, or Spearmint

Rhino – had applied to open a club on our local high street, and that we were almost entirely powerless to stop them. Thanks to a loophole in the law (one so large you wonder about the ability of politicians to read through the most simple of documents), lap-dancing clubs are licensed in exactly the same way as any pub or cafe. As a result, objections to licence applications can only be raised by a tiny section of the local community – those who live within 200m of the venue – and on only four grounds, as set out in the Licensing Act 2003 (these grounds are: public disorder, public nuisance, crime and disorder, and protection of children). As you will know if you have ever tried to object to, say, a pub's late licence, protesting on these grounds is difficult. How to prove that crime is up as a direct result of one nightspot? In the case of the lap-dancing clubs, moreover, they are rich enough – and smart enough – to ensure that they have sufficiently effective security to keep the street outside their venue quiet. All of which leaves residents who are uncomfortable with the club's main trade – the purchasing of a lap dance, performed by a naked woman – with no recourse. By law they cannot object on moral grounds, nor can they bring up the issue of gender equality and argue that such venues objectify women – in spite of the fact that this ruling puts local councils in breach of Gender Equality Duty 2007, which requires them to consider gender in all decision-making.

All this, however, is set to change, and in just a few weeks' time. Or that's the theory. In November 2007, a group called Object, which aims to challenge the objectification of women, launched a campaign called Stripping the Illusion. Supported by the Fawcett Society and others – the group quickly built an effective coalition of MPs, councillors and academics – Object began campaigning for a change in the law. It wanted lap-dancing clubs to be classed as sex-encounter establishments, as a Soho peep show might be; they would, in other words, need a new (and more expensive) licence to operate – one that would better take into account the feelings of local communities (because councils would at last be able to consider the

impact of such clubs on, say, nearby schools; these licences would also need to be renewed every year). Amazingly, just nine months later, the government announced that it would indeed draw up proposals on these lines. The Policing and Crime Bill, which includes this legislation, has now reached the committee stage in the Commons. It is expected to pass through the Lords and become law next month.

Only there is a catch. Or two. For one thing, the proposed legislation is not mandatory; it will be up to local authorities to decide whether they adopt it. Result: a postcode lottery that the lap-dancing industry will do its best to exploit. Campaigners point out that while many councils – perhaps the majority – will welcome the new legislation, some will resist. It is not only that councils are already under-resourced when it comes to licensing inspectors; in some smaller towns – Newquay, which has four clubs, would be a good example of this – councillors are convinced that lap dancing is beneficial to what they call the 'night-time economy'. The second flaw in the bill is that venues that host lap-dancing events less than once a month will be exempt. 'The government is under a lot of pressure from working men's clubs, which have occasional strip nights, to weaken the reforms,' says Sandrine Levêque of Object. 'But the conditions in those places, and especially in pubs that turn to irregular lap dancing as a way of improving revenues, is much worse than in the bigger venues. If anything, they need monitoring more, not less.'

Levêque and her colleagues are now working to put pressure on the government to amend the legislation,

and two Labour MPs, Lynda Waltho and Roberta Blackman-Woods, have tabled amendments. However, time is running out. 'The government is not very responsive at the moment,' says Levêque. 'I am not hugely optimistic.'

Is all this a fuss about nothing? After all, 300 (the number of clubs in the UK) is not that many, is it? And what harm, really, do lap-dancing clubs do? From the outside, with their inevitable strip of red carpet and their velvet cordons, they look a good deal more upmarket than most nightclubs. Girls like Lucy, surely, are in the minority. To the first three questions, the lap-dancing industry would answer: yes, no, and none, respectively. Its people would then tell you that the clubs' smart exteriors reflect what goes on inside – that they are, in fact, 'gentlemen's clubs' – and that this is why Lucy's testament is not to be trusted: a culture of 'respect' prevails in their professionally-run establishments and, as a result, its employees tend to be extremely happy in their work. 'I've worked in regular bars,' says Del Dhillon, the manager of Bandit Queen, a lap-dancing club in Dudley. 'Girls get molested in those places. This is a nicer environment. Here, you can leave your girlfriend at the bar, and no other gentleman is going to chat her up. That's why 15% of our customers are women. Me and my partner, we like a club like this, for a drink.'

Since Object came on the scene, the club owners have mobilised, aware that if the mood is turning against them in government, good public relations could be important. They established the Lap Dancing Association, a body that claims to represent a third of the industry, or 60 clubs, to 'improve industry standards'; its secretary is a woman, and when you call the PR company that acts on its behalf, you also deal with a young woman. Its president is Simon Warr, owner of the British end of the Spearmint Rhino chain. In 2002 undercover police officers found that dancers in Spearmint Rhino in Tottenham Court Road were making offers to customers with the 'intonation' of sex, and of cocaine; the club came close to losing its licence. At the magistrates court hearing, counsel for the Metropolitan Police described Warr as 'not fit and proper' to hold the licence. Unbowed, he is now high profile. It was Warr who last December gave evidence to a Culture, Media and Sport select committee in defence of lap dancing, though his arguments proved to be anything but convincing. To the amazement of both MPs and Peter Stringfellow, another witness, he insisted that lap dancing has nothing to do with sexual stimulation. (Stringfellow, whose own club only offered topless dancers before the arrival of Spearmint Rhino in the UK, rubbished this argument: 'Of course it's sexually stimulating,' he said.)

I meet Warr, a Kiwi who used to work in the motor industry, at Spearmint Rhino in Bournemouth. But before he and I talk, I speak to three of his dancers. These women, as you would expect, are keen to defend the work they do and furious that what they regard as patronising feminists seem bent on turning them into sex workers. However, their pride in their work does not extend to allowing me to use their real names. All three insist that I use their dance names. Two of them tell me that this is to avoid upsetting their parents. The family of the third knows full well what she does, but still: she would rather not tell me her real name.

So, about these new licences. They are not happy. 'People are going to start asking what extras we offer,' says Layla, 23. 'It will make the public think we're a brothel. It's irritating enough when customers ask that now. How dare these women fight a battle on our behalf without even talking to us first?' Her colleague, Jayda, agrees. 'We don't sell sex. It's a show. It's the same as acting. You're more protected in here than you are in a nightclub on a Saturday night. The security is amazing. No one misses a trick. You only have to say the word and they are gone, escorted out politely.' The third woman, Becky, 24, says: 'Customers are respectful. Some are scared of girls, so they find it so lovely that we'll sit down and talk to them. We're in control. There's rarely any drooling. They admire what we do. They feel it takes courage.'

Jayda, 35, is a single mother of two. She also happens to be a Muslim. She is

beautiful, and extremely soignée: crisp white shirt, dark jeans, soft sweater in Kelly green slung lightly about her shoulders. This job, she tells me, means that she can be with her children during the day, and work while they are asleep. She has been here four months. Given her background, would she ever have believed that she would one day end up working in a place like this? She smiles. 'No, it would have seemed preposterous. But you have an alter ego. It's quite hard to get your head around. As people, all of us are quite shy, retiring, insecure. My first night, I was on stage within 10 minutes. You switch off. You think: OK, I'm auditioning for a Broadway show. You don't see anything. You only see the lights.' Is the money good? Like her colleagues, she is infuriatingly vague about this. 'It's hard to say how much we take home. It's not a guaranteed income. You set targets for yourself. You think: tonight, I'm going to do 10 dances. I'm not going to the loo, or for a cigarette. Otherwise you might just sit and chat to someone fun all night.'

The women go off to eat the sandwiches that Warr has laid on for them, and he and I go into another corner to talk, on a black leather banquette that has been torn and then badly mended with what looks like duct tape. Lined up on either side of him are various beefy, dark-suited and apparently adoring male employees. Warr insists, first of all, that lap dancing is not a growth industry, in spite of the openings last year.

'Look at Bournemouth,' he says. 'No new clubs in the last five years.' But Bournemouth already has four such clubs: there is no room for more.

'Well, we need to make a distinction between clubs and premises that offer striptease.' Are the latter proliferating? 'Yes. They are exploiting a licensing loophole.' So he disapproves of those venues? 'Yes, because they have no proper safety facilities.' He does not, though, disapprove of striptease per se. So how does he feel about the change in the law? If his clubs are as suitably located and superbly run as he suggests, surely it won't be a problem for him, applying for the new licences? His only real worry is likely to be the increased financial costs. 'I'm shocked by it,' he says. 'And we are going to take this to court. We will push for a judicial review.' On what grounds? 'There has been no consultation, and the government pledged not to increase the bureaucratic burdens on business.'

If necessary, he says, the LDA will go the European Court of Human Rights (I've since spoken to a licensing barrister about this point and it is bluster; he has no grounds). The LDA's current plan of attack, however, is to demand grandfather rights for existing clubs, which would mean that they would be automatically granted the new licence, and on extended terms. But still: 'It's arse against the wall time for us. It's bloody unfair.'
It should be noted that Scotland is covered by different legislation on lap dancing than that which exists in England and Wales.

⇨ This information is an extract from a longer article which first appeared in *The Observer*, 8 March 2009. To read the full article, visit the *Guardian* archives at www.guardian. co.uk

Strip clubs to be licensed as Sex Encounter Venues

MPs vote to support lap dancing club licensing reforms

Tonight cross-party MPs voted overwhelmingly to support the Government's proposed changes to the way lap dancing clubs are licensed.[3] The new Shadow Home Secretary, Chris Grayling MP, spoke strongly in favour of the reforms, as did MPs Lynda Waltho, Roberta Blackman-Woods and Andrew Slaughter.

Lap dancing clubs are currently licensed under the 2003 Licensing Act in the same way as cafes and karaoke bars – with a Premises License. This lax regime has led to the number of lap dancing clubs in the UK doubling since 2004 to over 300 establishments, with local communities powerless to stop the spread.

Following an intensive nine month campaign led by the Fawcett Society and Object,[2] the Government is set to hand controls back to local people through the Policing and Crime Bill (PCB), by licensing lap dancing clubs as 'Sex Encounter Venues'.[4] This will enable local authorities to control the number and location of lap dancing clubs in their area, and give more local people a say in licensing decisions.

Dr Katherine Rake, Director of the Fawcett Society, commented on the vote by MPs:

'We welcome parliamentary support for these reforms. Lap dancing clubs are sexist and promote the degrading view that women are sex objects. All women have the right to be treated with dignity and respect and to feel safe in public spaces, yet areas around the clubs can become 'no-go' areas for women.

'The licensing reforms will enable local authorities to control and regulate lap dancing clubs, and enable local communities to claim back their high streets. It is crucial that Parliament ensures these reforms are robust, comprehensive, and deliver change to all local communities.'

Dr Sasha Rakoff, Director of Object, commented on the vote by MPs:

'We welcome the support shown by MPs for reform of lap dancing club licensing. The current system has acted as a green light to the industry – with a new lap dancing venue opening, on average, every week since May 2008 alone. It has also acted as a green light to sexism and 'sex object culture' – a culture in which women are increasingly portrayed as sex objects, not people.

'Changing the law will allow local councils to consider gender equality when licensing such venues and will restore democracy to the licensing process. Widespread support for the reforms – from the public, local councils, Local Government Association and women's rights organisations – has been reflected by today's debate which highlighted the need for thorough and far-reaching reforms.'

References

1   The Fawcett Society is the UK's leading campaign for women's rights. www.fawcettsociety.org.uk

2   Object is a women's rights organisation which campaigns against the objectification of women in the media and popular culture. www.object.org.uk

3   The Policing and Crime Bill, introduced by Home Secretary Jacqui Smith MP, received its second reading in the House of Commons on 19 January 2009. Key moments in the campaign included the following:

a. 18 June 2008: a 10 Minute

Rule Bill was introduced by Robert Blackman-Woods MP (City of Durham) calling for lap-dance clubs to be licensed as Sex Encounter Establishments. The Bill was unopposed and received cross-party support.

b. 18 June 2008: The Department for Culture, Media, and Sport began a consultation with all local authorities in England and Wales on whether they wanted greater powers to control and regulate lap dancing clubs. 75% of responding local authorities asked for such powers.

c. 21 September 2008: The Rt. Hon. Jacqui Smith announced at the Labour Party Conference that the Government would grant local people a greater say in stopping lap dancing clubs opening: http://www.labour.org.uk/jacqui_smith_speech,2008-09-21

d. 3 December 2008: Plans to tighten the licensing of lap dancing clubs were announced in the Queen's Speech.

4   Lap dancing clubs will be licensed as Sex Encounter Venues under the Local Government (Miscellaneous Provisions) Act 1982. This will require lap dancing club operators to obtain two licences; one for the sale of alcohol (Premises License), and a second for live visual performances given for the purpose of sexual stimulation, which are provided for the direct or indirect financial gain of the operator (Sex Encounter Venue licence).

19 January 2009

⇨ The above information is reprinted with kind permission from the Fawcett Society. Visit www.fawcettsociety.org.uk for more information.

© *Fawcett Society*

It's lap-dancing business as usual

The half-reforms of new licensing legislation play into the hands of club owners who are only too adept at manipulating the law

By Sandrine Levêque

A petition of 10,000 names to No 10. People taking to the streets to campaign in high streets nationwide. Monthly demos outside both political institutions and lap-dancing clubs. A cross-party coalition of women's organisations, women who've worked in lap-dancing clubs, councillors, parliamentarians, academics, local authorities and residents' associations. The list goes on – because the last year has seen a growing tide of frustration, led by Object and the Fawcett Society, about licensing laws that treat lap-dancing clubs in the same way as cafes or restaurants.

So it was a big, collective sigh of relief that welcomed the government's announcement that licensing reforms proposed by Object and Fawcett were to be included in the policing and crime bill. The reforms would see lap-dancing clubs licensed as sex-encounter venues – where entertainment for visual sexual stimulation is offered (much to the disgruntlement of the Lap Dancing Association, which vainly tried to argue this is not in its business plan).

Yet the relief was short-lived. Closer scrutiny of the draft bill reveals two gaping holes. First, the reforms will be optional for local councils. What will this mean? A postcode lottery in which whether you get a real say in the licensing of a lap-dancing club will depend on whether your local council has bothered to take up the new sex encounter venue category. It will mean a patchwork of licensing systems taking us right back to the previous licensing regime, in which lap-dancing club owners such as Peter Stringfellow brought pressure to bear on local councils to match weaker licensing in neighbouring areas. It will mean a ripple effect of displacement, as clubs move from councils that

have adopted the reforms to those that haven't.

Second, an exemption has been included for pubs and other venues that put on lap-dancing 'specials' less than once a month. It doesn't take a genius to work out that for clubs wanting to develop a 'stable of girls', as one club owner put it, touring exempted pubs and bars to put on lap-dancing events could actually be more lucrative than running a dedicated lap-dancing club. Add this to falling sales across the pub trade, and the scene is set for some serious use of new loopholes, all courtesy of the bill. It means that lap-dancing activities occurring in such settings – which often provide shoddy working conditions for performers – get the green light to keep doing so, while anyone who wishes to have their say in this will find themselves denied a voice.

The combination of these factors mean the bill will play right into the hands of an industry that is renowned for its manipulation of regulation. And it all amounts to a major opportunity being missed. The reforms offer a real chance to tip the balance from lap-dancing club owners back to ordinary people. For too long a 'markets never fail' approach has dominated both our economic and social thinking, hence 2003 licensing laws that essentially left lap-dancing clubs to 'self-regulate'. That model has been proved not to work. We need regulation that puts social priorities higher up the agenda and allows the social impact of venues – such as sexism – to be a major consideration in licensing. This will take strong licensing reforms, which are not at present on the table.

It's no surprise, then, that the huge tide of people calling for change are now waking up to the real implications of these half-hearted reforms. Individuals, organisations, local councils and parliamentarians are all calling on the government to toughen up the licensing reforms – by making them universal and removing the frequency-based exemption, as the recently published joint letter from councillors demonstrates.

The commitment of ministers to tackling inadequate licensing is to be welcomed. However, they would do well to heed the concerns of those warning them that partial reforms will seriously undermine what they are trying to achieve – a fair and socially just licensing system.

16 February 2009

Girls aged five 'sexualised by toys like Bratz dolls'

Young girls are being sexualised by inappropriate toys and magazines, a Holyrood committee was warned yesterday.

High-heeled slip-on shoes available for babies, sexual slogans printed on girls' underwear and magazines 'blurring' the lines by using child-like models, were highlighted to the equal opportunities committee.

And one of the most popular brands of dolls on shop shelves came in for particular criticism at the launch of the inquiry into the sexualisation of children.

Bratz dolls, which have been challenging Barbie for supremacy in the girls' toy market, were condemned by the NSPCC as the committee opened an inquiry into increasing levels of sexual imagery in goods aimed at children.

Tom Narducci, a senior consultant for the NSPCC, criticised the way dolls were dressed in short skirts and fishnet stockings and said they were sexualising girls as young as five.

The dolls were among a list of products and activities brought to the committee's attention.

There were also worries about young girls being given all-day beauty treatments with make-up and hair stylists, instead of traditional birthday parties.

But MGA Entertainments, which makes the Bratz dolls, hit back, saying that the problem had far more to do with what youngsters saw on television screens at home.

A spokesman said: 'In the end, Bratz are plastic dolls which are conservatively dressed by today's standards.

'The only people who have sexual images of them are adults, who have their own thoughts about these things.

'What is of far more concern is some of the live-action programmes where girls get their role models. These role models start out as 13- or

By David Maddox, Political Correspondent

14-year-old innocents and end up as promiscuous 16-year-olds or in nude pictorials.'

The committee also heard criticism of Playboy Bunny images being used on pencil cases and clothes marketed at young children.

> **High-heeled slip-on shoes available for babies, sexual slogans printed on girls' underwear and magazines 'blurring' the lines by using child-like models, were highlighted to the [Holyrood] equal opportunities committee**

There were fears that, at the extreme end, the social sexualisation of girls was being used by paedophiles to make their victims feel responsible for abuse. And it was also feared that it could force children into prostitution.

Mr Narducci warned that girls were effectively being trained to become sexual objects.

He said: 'The use of sexual imagery is now more pervasive than before and it does give a very disturbing perspective on girls and young women.

'For girls, it's all about being more attractive to a man. For boys, it's all about looking at girls as sexual objects because that is what they are being trained to become.'

Ed Mayo, the chief executive of Consumer Focus, warned that young people were 'more sexually confident now than they have ever been'.

He added that this sexualisation affected their school-work and led to many girls dropping out of the school system.

But there was anger that some organisations had refused to turn up to the committee meeting. They included Playboy, which sent in a submission; Asda, which has been under fire for selling clothes which sexualise young girls; the Scottish Grocers Federation and the Scottish Retail Consortium (SRC).

In a written submission, Playboy's chief executive, Christie Hefner, said that she would never allow licensees to use the Playboy Bunny image on children's products.

Fiona Moriarty, the SRC director, wrote: 'The SRC does not believe that much of the committee's focus is relevant to the retail sector – these issues are more aimed at the manufacturing and advertising sectors.'

But members of the round-table discussion disagreed. Nationalist MSP Sandra White called the SRC's response 'ridiculous'. Ms White added: 'They're absolving themselves completely, and that is absolutely wrong. I'm very disappointed with their attitude.'

What next?

The equal opportunities committee was yesterday attempting to 'test the water' on the issue of whether young children are being sexualised by products.

The committee will now decide whether to take the issue forward as a full-blown inquiry when it next discusses its work programme.

'The use of sexual imagery is now more pervasive than before'

The committee's Conservative convener, Margaret Mitchell, told The Scotsman that she believes there is a mood among members to take the discussions to a more formal stage. 'I think the members of the committee found it a very positive and interesting meeting,' she said.

'There is a lot of material to work on, but there is also a lack of proper research, which the committee could carry out. This is a subject that concerns people widely and one I think we are keen to pursue, but that ultimately is for the committee members to decide.'

If the committee does hold a full inquiry into the issue, this can potentially form the background to new legislation, or could see the committee calling on the Scottish Government to take certain steps to tackle the problem.

It is likely organisations such as Asda, Playboy or retail industry representatives who declined to come to yesterday's meeting will be called on again to give evidence to justify some of their commercial activities.

11 February 2009

© *The Scotsman*

Teen mags 'cause early sexualisation'

Teenage magazines have been blasted for sexualising their young readers by the UK Government's consumer watchdog

Teenage magazines have been blasted for sexualising their young readers by the UK Government's consumer watchdog.

Ed Mayo, chief executive of Consumer Focus, said magazines which are read by children as young as 10 or 11 contained content which would shock their parents.

An example is contained in the latest edition of *Sugar* magazine, with an average reader age of 14, which features a spread entitled 'Is it a crush or are you gay?'. *Bliss* magazine, whose average reader is 15 years old, has previously invited girls to send in photographs of themselves to be judged on looks in a competition called 'How Sexy Am I?'.

Campaigners say the 'normalisation' of the magazines' sexual ethos has contributed to soaring teenage pregnancy rates, warning that the current regulatory system is 'toothless'.

A study of the magazines conducted by the *Sunday Telegraph* found that they contained sexually explicit material that could be in breach of industry guidelines.

The magazine industry is self-regulated, with the Teenage Magazine Arbitration Panel (TMAP) existing to ensure that 'the sexual content of teenage magazines is presented in a responsible and appropriate manner'.

Its chairman, Dr Fleur Fisher, said: 'Any complaints we receive from readers are carefully checked against our guidelines, and we respond accordingly.'

However, critics argue that few parents are aware of the TMAP, which has ruled on just three complaints since it was launched in 1996. In the past three years it has only received one complaint.

Mr Mayo said: 'There is no doubt that some of these magazines are responsible for the early sexualisation of children.'

Sue Palmer, an educational consultant and the author of *Toxic Childhood*, said: 'The reality is that children as young as 10 read these magazines, and what they are being exposed to is often horrific and entirely inappropriate.

'The very blatantly sexual ethos expressed in them is becoming normalised among young girls. Then we wonder why we have such high teenage pregnancy rates and a booming ladette culture.'

21 March 2009

⇨ The above information is reprinted with kind permission from ciNews. Visit www.cinews.co.uk for more information.

© *ciNews*

⇨ In the UK, prostitution itself is not illegal but there are a number of offences linked to it. For example, it is an offence to control a prostitute for gain or to keep a brothel. (page 1)

⇨ Prostitution is sometimes referred to as 'the oldest profession', as it meets the natural urges of humans in return for money, and is often claimed to be as old as civilisation itself. (page 1)

⇨ There are estimated to be around 80,000 people involved in prostitution in the UK. (page 2)

⇨ 9% of men in the UK have paid for sex, and 4.2% have done so in the last five years. In the 1990s, the number of men buying sex in the UK doubled. (page 3)

⇨ 52% of women in street prostitution were under 18 when they first worked in prostitution. (page 3)

⇨ Almost six in ten (59%) people surveyed by Ipsos MORI agree with the statement that 'prostitution is a perfectly reasonable choice that women should be free to make', while a quarter (27%) disagree. (page 4)

⇨ 50% of people surveyed by Ipsos MORI felt that the selling of sex by women should be legal, with 42% thinking it should be illegal. This compared with 51% of respondents who felt that the purchase of sex by men should be legal and 43% who felt it should be illegal. (page 4)

⇨ A US survey of 119 women engaged in prostitution reported that performing prostitution was a negative and/or traumatic experience for the women 90% of the time. (page 5)

⇨ 18% of people surveyed said they would definitely consider having sex for money if the amount was large enough, and a further 13% said they would consider the offer. (page 6)

⇨ The grooming of schoolgirls as young as 12 into prostitution by gangs of men is a growing national problem, a senior MP has warned. (page 11)

⇨ Germany legalised prostitution in 2003. The subsequent effects of the legislation have been concerning. Several German NGOs now estimate that as many as 75% of women in brothels are from abroad. (page 13)

⇨ New measures announced by the Government would mean that men would be breaking the law if they paid for sex with a woman trafficked into the UK or working for a pimp, regardless of whether the man was aware the woman was forced into prostitution. (page 14)

⇨ The US state department claims that between 600,000 and 800,000 people are trafficked for forced labour or sex worldwide every year; Unicef says a million children and young people are trafficked each year. (page 17)

⇨ Almost 40% of the male population used pornographic websites in 2005. British Internet users search for 'porn' online more than anyone else in the English-speaking world. (page 19)

⇨ In December 2008, a report found that 100% of sixth form girls surveyed were angry, upset or offended by images of women in *Nuts*, *Zoo* and the *Daily Sport*, compared to only 11% of sixth form boys, although one-fifth of male respondents thought such pictures encouraged them to view women as objects. (page 19)

⇨ Strictly speaking, legally-acceptable pornographic magazines displayed on the top shelf of a newsagent can be sold legally to anyone of any age. They are sold on the top shelf and to over-18s only by convention. (page 21)

⇨ It has become illegal in most of the UK to own extreme pornographic images. A new law came into force making it a criminal offence to possess the images in England, Wales and Northern Ireland. A similar law is proposed in Scotland. (page 22)

⇨ Every second $3,075,64 is being spent on pornography. (page 26)

⇨ Every 39 minutes a new pornographic video is being created in the United States. (page 26)

⇨ 66% of young people say that they find out about sex, love and relationships through the media. (page 27)

⇨ 63% of girls say that they would rather be glamour models than teachers or doctors. (page 30)

⇨ *FHM* has the highest circulation of any lads' mag. (page 31)

⇨ The lap-dancing industry estimates it employs 10,000 women. (page 32)

⇨ In 2008, a lap-dancing club opened in Britain almost every week. (page 33)

⇨ The number of lap dancing clubs in the UK has doubled since 2004 to over 300 establishments. (page 36)

GLOSSARY

Criminalisation

In terms of prostitution, this refers to making both the buying and selling of sex illegal, so both a prostitute and her client would be breaking the law. This policy is in force throughout most of the United States.

Criminalising demand

This suggests that prostitution exists due to gender inequality and therefore is best combatted by making the buying of sex a criminal offence. Therefore men who use prostitutes would be breaking the law, but the prostitutes themselves would not. This is currently the law in Sweden.

Decriminalisation

There is a debate surrounding the legal status of prostitution, with some suggesting that if criminal offences relating to prostitution were removed this would improve the safety and working conditions of women within the sex industry. However, critics say that this has not been the case in other countries such as New Zealand which have already decriminalised prostitution.

Grooming

Befriending a child with the intention of first gaining their trust and then sexually abusing them. A senior Labour MP recently warned that girls as young as 12 were being groomed for prostitution by gangs of men.

Kerb crawling

Kerb crawling means driving a car very slowly alongside areas where prostitutes are known to look for clients, for the purpose of engaging their services. Kerb crawling has been a criminal offence in England and Wales since 1985.

Lads' mags

A term used to describe magazines geared towards 'lad culture', such as *Zoo*, *Nuts*, *Loaded* and *FHM*. These magazines tend to focus heavily on sexy photoshoots with celebrities as their main selling point, leading some critics to claim that they are little more than pornography.

Legalisation

In terms of prostitution, this refers to making prostitution and related activities legal, thereby allowing greater Government control and regulation. This is the situation in the Netherlands, where brothels must meet conditions regarding location, management and workplace standards before being granted a license.

Pimp

This is a slang word which can be used as a noun ('a pimp') or a verb ('to pimp'). A pimp is a person, usually a man, who controls a prostitute, arranging what services she offers, when and to whom she offers them and taking a percentage of her profits. To 'pimp' someone is to control them in this way.

Pornography

The depiction of explicit sexual content for the purpose of sexually stimulating the person viewing it. Pornography can exist in any medium, including print, film and online. There is much debate surrounding pornography, with some people feeling it is immoral and should be censored and others feeling that it objectifies women by catering to stereotypically male sexual fantasies. However, in spite of these views pornography is a large and lucrative market. The possession of pornography classed as 'extreme', depicting acts of sexual violence, has recently been made illegal in the UK. Some other types of pornography are legally available but are age-restricted.

Prostitution

Also called 'the sex trade', prostitution describes the offering and provision of sexual services for financial gain. While it is not illegal in the UK, there are a number of offences linked to it, such as keeping a brothel or controlling a prostitute for gain. Most prostitutes are women selling their services to men, although there are exceptions. Estimates suggest around 80,000 people are involved in prostitution in the UK.

Sexualisation

The process of becoming more focussed upon or geared towards sex and sexuality. Some would suggest that society as a whole is becoming 'sexualised' through the prevalence of sexual images in advertising and brands like the Playboy logo. There is also concern over the sexualisation of children and young people, with mini-skirted dolls and clothes bearing slogans such as 'porn star' being marketed at very young children.

Sex worker

Someone who works within the sex industry. It is often used instead of 'prostitute', which many within the sex industry feel has negative connotations and stigmatises them unfairly. 'Sex worker' can also refer to other sex industry workers, such as those employed within the pornography industry.

Trafficking

The transport and/or trade of people from one area to another, usually for the purpose of forcing them into labour or prostitution. According to 2005 statistics from the International Labour Organisation, 2.45 million people are victims of trafficking annually, of which 50% are children.

INDEX

Additional Resources

Other Issues *titles*

If you are interested in researching further some of the issues raised in *Selling Sex*, you may like to read the following titles in the **Issues** series:

⇨ Vol. 173 *Sexual Health* (ISBN 978 1 86168 487 5)

⇨ Vol. 170 *Body Image and Self-Esteem* (ISBN 978 1 86168 484 4)

⇨ Vol. 168 *Privacy and Surveillance* (ISBN 978 1 86168 472 1)

⇨ Vol. 167 *Our Human Rights* (ISBN 978 1 86168 471 4)

⇨ Vol. 166 *Marriage and Cohabitation* (ISBN 978 1 86168 470 7)

⇨ Vol. 164 *The AIDS Crisis* (ISBN 978 1 86168 468 4)

⇨ Vol. 163 *Drugs in the UK* (ISBN 978 1 86168 456 1)

⇨ Vol. 160 *Poverty and Exclusion* (ISBN 978 1 86168 453 0)

⇨ Vol. 158 *The Internet Revolution* (ISBN 978 1 86168 451 6)

⇨ Vol. 157 *The Problem of Globalisation* (ISBN 978 1 86168 444 8)

⇨ Vol. 155 *Domestic Abuse* (ISBN 978 1 86168 442 4)

⇨ Vol. 154 *The Gender Gap* (ISBN 978 1 86168 441 7)

⇨ Vol. 137 *Crime and Anti-Social Behaviour* (ISBN 978 1 86168 389 2)

⇨ Vol. 134 *Customers and Consumerism* (ISBN 978 1 86168 386 1)

⇨ Vol. 133 *Teen Pregnancy and Lone Parents* (ISBN 978 1 86168 379 3)

⇨ Vol. 132 *Child Abuse* (ISBN 978 1 86168 378 6)

⇨ Vol. 130 *Homelessness* (ISBN 978 1 86168 376 2)

⇨ Vol. 121 *The Censorship Debate* (ISBN 978 1 86168 354 0)

⇨ Vol. 99 *Exploited Children* (ISBN 978 1 86168 313 7)

⇨ Vol. 89 *Refugees* (ISBN 978 1 86168 290 1)

For more information about these titles, visit our website at www.independence.co.uk/publicationslist

Useful organisations

You may find the websites of the following organisations useful for further research:

⇨ **24dash:** www.24dash.com

⇨ **CARE:** www.care.org.uk

⇨ **ciNews:** www.cinews.co.uk

⇨ **Eaves:** www.eaves4women.co.uk

⇨ **Fawcett Society:** www.fawcettsociety.org.uk

⇨ **Ipsos MORI:** www.ipsos-mori.com

⇨ **New Statesman:** www.newstatesman.com

⇨ **Object:** www.object.org.uk

⇨ **openDemocracy:** www.opendemocracy.net

⇨ **Pinsent Masons LLP:** www.out-law.com

⇨ **politics.co.uk:** www.politics.co.uk

⇨ **Red Pepper:** www.redpepper.org.uk

⇨ **Women's Support Project:** www.womenssupportproject.co.uk

ACKNOWLEDGEMENTS

The publisher is grateful for permission to reproduce the following material.

While every care has been taken to trace and acknowledge copyright, the publisher tenders its apology for any accidental infringement or where copyright has proved untraceable. The publisher would be pleased to come to a suitable arrangement in any such case with the rightful owner.

Chapter One: Prostitution

Prostitution, © Adfero, *Prostitution: a summary,* © Fawcett Society, *Public's views on prostitution,* © Ipsos MORI, *Prostitution – fact or fiction?,* © Women's Support Project, *'Callous' sex trafficking gang jailed,* © 24dash.com, *I'm a sex worker – don't take away my livelihood,* © Guardian Newspapers Ltd 2009, *Schoolgirls lured into prostitution, warns MP,* © 24dash. com, *International approaches to prostitution,* © CARE, *New prostitution laws 'unenforceable',* © Adfero, *New laws will make sex workers more vulnerable,* © openDemocracy.net, *Human trafficking and the sex industry,* © CARE, *The myth of trafficking,* © New Statesman.

Chapter Two: Pornography

Pornography, © Eaves, *The law and pornography,* © CARE, *Ban on extreme images comes into force,* © Pinsent Masons LLP, *Criminalising extreme porn,* © New Statesman, *Jane Austen and the case for extreme porn,* © Times Newspapers Ltd, *Change society and porn will change too,* © Red Pepper.

Chapter Three: Sexualising Society

Sex object culture, © Object, *MPs want age ratings for lads' mags,* © Sky News, *Lads' mags,* © Object, *Why lads' mags have a shelf life,* © Telegraph Group Ltd, London 2009, *Should lap dancing be run out of town?,* © Guardian Newspapers Ltd 2009, *Strip clubs to be licensed as Sex Encounter Venues,* © Fawcett Society, *It's lap dancing business as usual,* © Guardian Newspapers Ltd 2009, *Girls aged five 'sexualised by toys like Bratz dolls',* © The Scotsman, *Teen mags 'cause early sexualisation',* © ciNews.

Photographs

Flickr: pages 11 (Valeria C Preisler); 17 (michael_swan); 34 (Richard Riley).
Stock Xchng: pages 15 (Martin Boose); 19 (Paulo Correa); 22 (Ariel da Silva Parreira); 28 (Armando Apollo); 39 (loleia).
Wikimedia Commons: page 14 (Kay Chernush for the U.S. State Department).

Illustrations

Pages 1, 10, 25: Angelo Madrid; pages 7, 16, 30, 37: Don Hatcher; pages 8, 24, 29: Simon Kneebone; pages 13, 21, 35, 38: Bev Aisbett.

And with thanks to the team: Mary Chapman, Sandra Dennis, Claire Owen and Jan Sunderland.

Lisa Firth
Cambridge
May, 2009